Black Kid, White School: What They Don't Teach Your Black Child

Volume 1

By Joel I. Plummer

©2025 by Joel I. Plummer

All rights reserved.

No part of this book may be reproduced or transmitted in any form or by any means, electronic or mechanical, including photocopying and recording, or by any information storage and retrieval system, without permission in writing from the author and publisher.

Cover illustration by Alexis ☽ Plummer

Plummer Media & Entertainment, LLC.
Plainfield, NJ
www.joelplummer.com

Paperback ISBN: 978-0-9744490-3-6

To Alexis, Morgan, and Mason,

I may not always be with you physically, but I hope the information in this book provides you with a lifetime of protection against anyone who tries to make you feel small. You come from giants, and may this book always serve as a reminder of that.

Introduction vii

Lesson 1: Africa...1

Lesson 2: Slavery 15

Lesson 3: Ending Slavery 49

Lesson 4: Reconstruction and Jim Crow 57

Lesson 5: Black Resistance and Resiliency...........83

Conclusion 119

Glossary..121

References 125

About the Author 151

Introduction

Almost all Black children in America go to White schools. I do not mean, though, that nearly all Black children enter school buildings each day where the majority of their classmates are White. A small number of Black students attend schools with a majority White student body. The typical Black student in America, however, goes to a school that is 70.9% non-White. Meanwhile, the typical White American student goes to a school that is 66.4% White and only 8% Black (Orfield & Pfleger, 2024). Nevertheless, whether a Black student is in the minority or majority of their school's population, both of their schools subject them to a Eurocentric educational experience.

Regardless of their schools' racial composition, all Black students have to deal with the reality of being taught by people who often have no direct connection to their culture:

> Seventy-nine percent of American teachers are White, while Black teachers only make up 8% of the nation's teaching force (National Council on Educational Statistics, 2020). Given America's still mostly segregated housing patterns, it is likely that many of these teachers have had little meaningful contact with Black people during their lives. As a result, White teachers' understanding of Black children is not based on real-life experiences with them but rather on a hodgepodge of information and images from pop culture. It is no surprise, then, that some teachers subconsciously bring negative perceptions of Black children to the classroom" (Plummer, 2020).

The Black student in a majority White school has the double burden of being placed outside of the school's curriculum and its social structure. One Black parent wrote this about the dilemma of choosing the right school for her child:

> This is the constant "head versus heart" rumination black parents make on a regular basis. Even when there are no major racist incidents, your child faces an assault of daily challenges: not having teachers who look like them, the isolation of being an "only," which often comes with social exclusion, the burden of being the representative minority who has to explain or represent all black people all the time. In these environments, black children can never come to school with the freedom to just learn. They are forced to carry so much more with them every day along with their backpacks" (Allers, 2019).

Moreover, even when Black students have Black teachers, principals, and superintendents, they often implement a Eurocentric curriculum that varies little from that of their White counterparts. Therefore, regardless of the people in the classroom they are sitting in, most Black students receive an educational experience designed for White students (Plummer, 2020). So, even in the Blackest of neighborhoods, Black students are still effectively attending White schools.

Most of my educational experience involves teaching and mentoring teenage students. By the time students reach my high school history classes, they usually have developed a great apathy or disdain for history. I rarely have classes where the majority of students already enjoy history. The most common complaint I hear from my students is that history is a collection of old and irrelevant stories that have no bearing on their lives, presently or in the future.

My students' lack of interest in history is quite understandable. As modest as people try to be, we like hearing about ourselves. Think about it this way: A group of friends has a conversation at the same time and in the same place every day. However, every day, the conversation is about the events of only one person in that group. As interesting as the person may be, eventually, the other people in the group will also want to discuss what is happening in their lives. They will ultimately grow uninterested in the group's discussion and leave if they cannot; this is what schools put Black students through. They constantly study various aspects of the history of White Western Europeans and White Americans. While important and interesting, being taught the history of White people year after year becomes like that conversation that is always about the same person and their activities every day. In the above scenario, discussion group members can leave once they tire of discussing everything except themselves. However, children in school have no such luxury. They cannot just get fed up and walk out of class, so they mentally check out. They learn how to minimally engage in their perceived meaningless history classes just enough to earn good grades that will keep their parents happy.

After a decade or so of learning about people other than themselves in any significant way, they come to my class expecting to have the same conversation that they have been unwillingly forced to participate in for the past ten years. Though normal teenage behavior almost mandates a cool indifference to just about everything, I have found that it is relatively easy to get Black youth interested in Black History and, subsequently, the history of other people. Despite their bias against history, teenagers are remarkably curious about the world around them. That curiosity is the key to awakening Black students' interest in history and, consequently, themselves. My students mentally check back into history class when I begin teaching them about their own history. I teach that history is not merely about memorizing random stories of people who died hundreds of years ago. Instead, history is a means of studying the past to understand yourself and your potential. It also gives you the power to understand everything that currently surrounds you and to predict what will happen in the future, as humans tend to repeat their behaviors century after century.

Teaching Black students about their own history can have a significant impact on their attitudes and self-perception. They feel more pride in themselves, see more possibilities for their future, and are exposed to a larger world beyond their immediate surroundings. However, it is important to recognize that learning Black history is not a cure-all for all Black youths' problems. Although it may not solve every problem, it can help them appreciate what they have today and expand their vision for what is possible in the future. Black students who know their own history gain a kind of confidence that only comes from knowing they stand on a spectacular foundation of achievement and greatness.

Some may argue that some subjects and details are missing from this book, and I would not disagree. Few reasonable people, though, will argue that any of the information I have included is unnecessary. This book is meant to supplement a comprehensive study of history. My primary goal is to fill in the gaps in the reader's preexisting knowledge. I hope this book inspires Black parents and their children to research and explore more detailed studies of the topics I only briefly touch upon in *Black Kid, White School: What They Don't Teach Your Black Child*.

This book is organized as a series of questions and answers that a newer student of Black history might ask if they were in my classroom. While readers can go through the book from start to finish, it is also designed for those who may not want to spend hours studying history at once. For those readers, they can open to any random page and read a question and answer for a quick, meaningful history lesson without feeling overwhelmed by a long read. In short, this book is designed to cater to readers who are used to absorbing quick bursts of information similar to what they receive from TikTok, Instagram, or YouTube Shorts videos.

The ultimate goal of this book is summed up in one word: protection. This book's objective is to give Black parents and their children an intellectual vaccination that protects their minds from the disease of White supremacy that pervades their schools. To be clear, I do not intend this book to provide Black parents with all the historical information they will ever need to teach their children. Reading this book will not qualify you to teach a history course at your local college. However, it will make the reader more knowledgeable than most people and give Black children a superior understanding of themselves and the world around them. It will also make Black children more capable of recognizing and challenging their schools' intentional and unintentional attacks on their intellect, beauty, culture, ideologies, and value as human beings. As parents, we cannot live our children's lives for them, but we can provide them with the strongest base to stand on as they face the challenges of Black life in America. I hope this book is a valuable tool in constructing that foundation.

Lesson 1: Africa

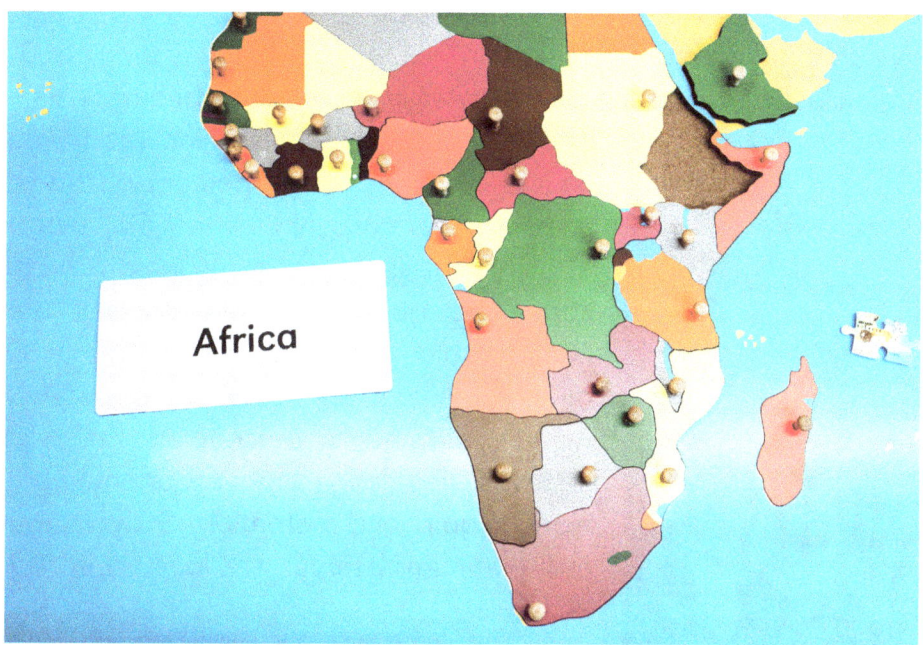

Core Concepts

- Africa is the birthplace of all humanity and civilization, where Black Africans built advanced societies long before European societies developed.
- West African empires such as Ghana, Mali, and Songhai were rich, powerful, and highly educated, with schools that attracted global scholars.
- Western education often erases this history by starting Africa's story with slavery, which distorts Black identity and denies Black students knowledge of their ancestral greatness.

Language in the Lesson

Africa - The world's most resource-rich continent and the birthplace of humanity.
Great Rift Valley – The region where some of the oldest modern human fossils were found.
Kemet – The original name for Egypt, meaning "the black land."
Mitochondrial Eve – A nickname for the African woman whose DNA is shared by all humans today.
Songhai, Mali, Ghana – Major West African empires with wealth, governance, and scholarship.
Timbuktu – A West African city known for its ancient books and universities.

Q: What is Africa?
A: *Africa* is a massive continent containing 54 countries. It is 5,000 miles long, 4,600 miles wide, and 11.73 million square miles, making it the second-largest continent behind Asia. For context, the United States, with Alaska included, is about 3.8 million square miles. About 10 percent of the world's population lives there and speaks over 1,500 languages (Britannica, 2019). Africa is the most resource-rich continent on Earth, containing deposits of oil, copper, diamonds, bauxite, lithium, gold, timber, and fruits. Nearly 30% of the world's mineral reserves are in Africa alone. Twelve percent of the world's oil and 8 percent of the world's natural gas reserves are also on the continent. Forty percent of the world's gold and potentially 90 percent of its chromium and platinum reserves are located in Africa (Environment, 2017).

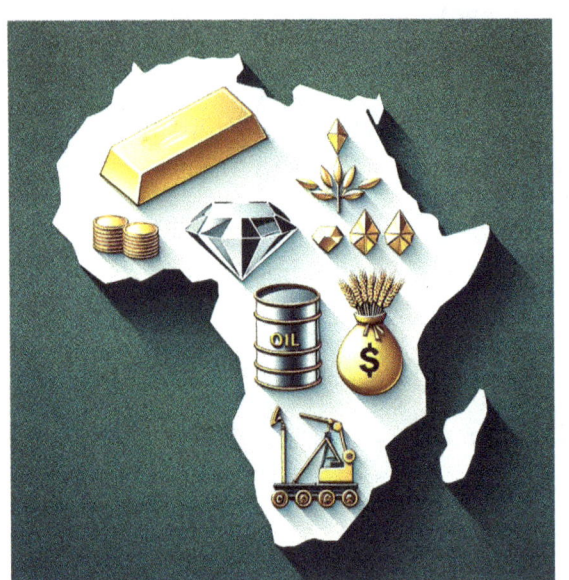

Q: Where did human life begin?
A: All of the oldest human fossils have been discovered in Africa. Scholars have dated these fossils as old as 14 million years. Modern humans, known as homo-sapiens, were present in Africa around 200,000 years ago in what is now called the **Great Rift Valley**, located in eastern Africa. In this area, researchers discovered one of the oldest nearly complete skulls of a clearly modern human, which they dated as 160,000 years old and named Idaltu. Additionally, geneticists have been able to trace all human DNA back to a single African female from approximately 200,000 years ago, whom they have nicknamed "**Mitochondrial Eve**." This term refers to the most recent common ancestor of all humans alive today, from whom all humans descend in an unbroken line through their mothers. So, everyone on Earth is connected to this singular Black woman through their DNA (Bates et al., 2017).

Q: What was happening in Europe when these early modern humans were walking about in Africa?
A: When modern-day humans were already living in Africa, Neanderthals populated Europe (Bates et al., 2017). Neanderthals were a species similar to humans and lived in Europe and Asia, but they

Fig. 1
A San man in Namibia.
Note. Source: (Beatty, 2006).

eventually went extinct 40,000 years ago. Today, some people in Europe and Asia may still possess up to 3% Neanderthal DNA (European Commission, 2022).

Q: If human life began in Africa, why don't all people look the same worldwide?

A: The diversity of the genetic human traits originating from African ancestry is remarkable. It boasts the most varied genetic pool on the planet (Gomez et al., 2014). Africans' physical characteristics range from dark to light skin, hair that can be straight or curly, and even blonde. Interestingly, even epicanthic fold eyes (the shape of the eyes commonly associated with Far East Asians) can also be found in the older southern regions of the African continent. Think of Africans as the source code from which all human life is based, but as Africans traveled across the world, they experienced changes in diet, climate, and environment that altered their appearances (Ghose, 2014).

Q: Where did human civilization begin?

A: The oldest civilizations in the world originated in Africa. Human life evolved and developed in Africa for thousands of years before eventually spreading to other parts of the world. Therefore, it is not surprising that Africans also created the first civilizations.

Fig. 2
Children in the Solomon Islands in the South Pacific Ocean.
Note. Source: (Sebastian, 2012).

Q: Wait a minute! Isn't Mesopotamia considered the "Cradle of Civilization?" So, weren't the first civilizations in Asia?

A: Unfortunately, some schools still teach students that humans did not develop civilizations until they left Africa. This confusion arises from the belief that only large and complex societies qualify as civilizations, which is not true. Urbanization and civilization are not the same thing (Supreme Understanding, 2013). People achieve civilization when their society is no longer concerned with mere survival. At that point, their society is stable and persistent, and they begin engaging in activities like art and religious reflection (Karenga, 2002). Africans reached that level of development many thousands of years before leaving the continent, signifying they had settled and established permanent societies (Bates et al., 2017).

Q: What proof is there that early Africans engaged in high-level thinking?
A: For many years, the oldest known art was believed to be the 35,000-year-old cave paintings discovered in France. However, researchers have recently unearthed even older evidence of artistic expression in Blombos Cave in South Africa. Specifically, they discovered 77,000-year-old artwork and paint kits, indicating that early Africans were significantly more advanced than past scholars had acknowledged (Bates et al., 2017). In the Nile Valley, between 7,000 and 4,500 B.C., Africans created stone tools, domesticated animals and plants, crafted jewelry, and made ceramic containers and pottery (Metropolitan Museum of Art, 2023). Scholars' earliest evidence of human writing is from Africans in Egypt in 3200 B.C. in the form of small tags that indicated property ownership (Bates et al., 2017).

Fig. 3
Intentional artistic patterns carved into stone over 70,000 years ago in Blombos Cave, South Africa.
Note. Source: (Henshilwood, 2014).

Q: When did Africans establish the first complex societies on the continent?
A: Africans formed complex societies west of the Nile River between 4,800 and 4,200 B.C. These people eventually traveled east and established the kingdoms of Nubia and **Kemet** (Egypt) (Bates et al., 2017). Nubia, located south of Egypt, was Egypt's rival, collaborator, and conqueror at different times. It is important to note that, as powerful as Egypt was, Nubia controlled the gold in the area and access to the interior of Africa (Bates et al., 2017).

Q: What is Kemet?
A: Kemet is the name Africans used for the ancient land that the Greeks would later name Egypt. It means "the black land" or "the black people of the land (Hilliard, 1992). For simplification, though, we will use Egypt in this book, as most new history students are more familiar with that name.

Q: Were ancient Egyptians Black?
A: The simple answer is yes. Thousands of years after Egypt's founding, it experienced large-scale invasions from Europeans and Asians and became a multiracial society. Still, they were Black when the Egyptians created most of the things for which they are most famous (e.g., pyramids, the Sphinx, mathematical and philosophical knowledge). Sometimes, modern people are confused about the identity of ancient Egyptians because they are unaware of what East Africans look like. Sujan Kumar Dass writes:

> Despite any controversy from the Eurocentrists, the evidence clearly shows us that the ancient Badarians, Somalians, Ethiopians, and Egyptians were ALL Black, African people, but they didn't all look like West Africans. They looked like East Africans. East Africans are very diverse, but many of them, like the Samburu of Kenya, have straight, narrow noses and sharp cheekbones, but jet Black skin" (Supreme Understanding, 2013, p. 384).

Cheikh Anta Diop is renowned for arguing that the ancient Egyptians were distinctly black Africans. He supported his claim by referencing various forms of evidence, including blood tests, melanin dosage tests, bone measurements, Egyptian art, eyewitness accounts, and the cultural similarities between Egypt and other African regions. According to Diop, all these factors indicate that the Egyptians were indeed black Africans (Karenga, 2002). The people who inhabit Egypt today are not the same as those who inhabited ancient Egypt 5,000 years ago. Because Egyptians sometimes did not look like some people's stereotype of an African, they erroneously assumed that ancient Egyptians had always been multiracial. The first Asian invasion of Egypt occurred during the 13th-17th dynasties (1550-1170 B.C.), when Egypt was already thousands of years old. Europeans from Greece and Rome did not invade until 332 B.C. and 30 B.C., respectively. Egypt's present-day multiracial population comprises descendants of Assyrians, Syrians, Persians, and Europeans, who intermarried with the native Black population of the area many years after Black Africans founded Egypt (Browder, 2007).

Despite any controversy from the Eurocentrists, the evidence clearly shows us that the ancient Badarians, Somalians, Ethiopians, and Egyptians were ALL Black.

Q: Why is there so much focus on Egypt?
A: Throughout history, Africans from all over the continent achieved remarkable feats. For instance, around 8,000 years ago, people in what is now the Democratic Republic of the Congo (formerly

Zaire) developed their own numerical system. Similarly, the Yoruba in present-day Nigeria created a number system based on 20 (Blatch, 2013). The Dogon in Mali were aware of Saturn's rings, Jupiter's moons, and the Sirius B star years before European astronomers (Chinguwo, 2008). Scholars used to think that humans first began working with iron in Turkey in 1,500 B.C. However, they have now discovered that Africans developed ironworking simultaneously. By 700 B.C., Africans in what is now Chad, Nigeria, and Mali had all engaged in ironwork (Bates et al., 2017). Nevertheless, Egypt was the most impressive civilization of the ancient world.

Fig. 4
Artist's interpretation of Sirius A and the much smaller Sirius B stars.
Note. Source: (NASA, ESA, and G. Bacon (STScI), 2005).

Q: What were some of the accomplishments of Africans in ancient Egypt?

A: Africans in Egypt created math textbooks that covered multiplication, division, fractions, and formulas to determine the area and volume of shapes. They also created algebraic formulas that helped them predict when the Nile River would flood and to what degree. Egyptians knew a circle was 360 degrees and estimated Pi to be 3.16. Egyptians charted the movement of the sun, stars, and moon cycles. They also figured out that a year is 365 days and divided the year into 12 periods (Blatch, 2013). They made clocks powered by moving water and sundials to tell the time of day (Cotterell et al., 1986). Egyptians were the first to write on a paper-like substance (Lee Hayes May, 2018). Egyptians diagnosed and treated more than 200 diseases, conducted surgeries, and had tools to listen to the inside of bodies. Regarding religious philosophies, the Egyptians were the first to develop a monotheistic religion, centuries before Judaism (National Geographic, 2016). They also introduced humanity to the spiritual concepts of life after death and resurrection. (Karenga, 2002).

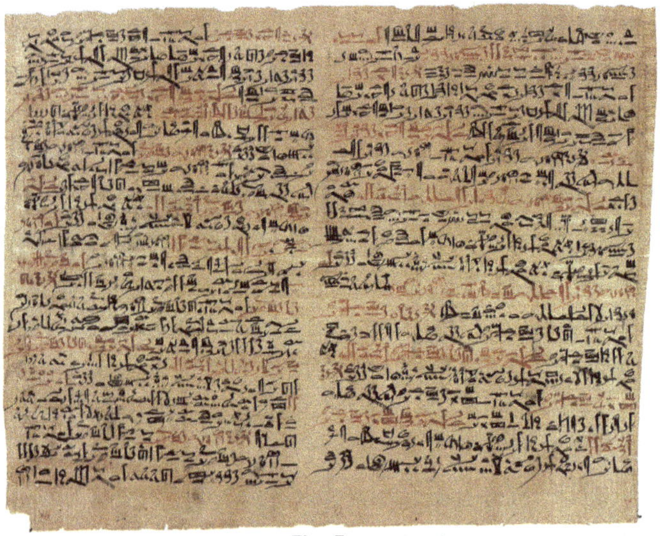

Fig. 5
An Egyptian papyrus from 1600 B.C. that describes medical treatments for 48 types of ailments.
Note. Source: (NASA, ESA, and G. Bacon (STScI), 2005).

Egyptians invented irrigation systems and mastered animal domestication, enabling them to establish a continuous society. They became masters in cloth weaving, woodworking, pottery, shipbuilding, glassmaking, leatherwork, and mining gold, silver, copper, brass, and bronze. Egyptians also developed the necessary tools to shape and refine these resources, such as hammers, mallets, saws, and drills (Karenga, 2002).

Egyptians are most famous for their massive stone work projects, such as the Great Sphinx and the Pyramids at Giza. In *Nile Valley Contributions to Civilization*, Tony Browder explains how awe-inspiring the Great Pyramid is. This massive structure is composed of 2.5 million stones that weigh an average of 2.5 tons each. Some of the stones weigh up to 70 tons each. The base of the Great Pyramid is seven city blocks in size. It is equivalent to a 45-story modern building and contains enough stone to build 30 Empire State Buildings (Browder, 2007). It was the tallest building on Earth for 4,000 years (Bates et al., 2017).

Fig. 6
The Pyramids at Giza in Egypt.
Note. Source: (Liberato, 2007).

Q: Did slaves build the ancient Egyptian pyramids?
A: Too often, people believe that the pyramids in Egypt were built by slaves, particularly Hebrew slaves, as depicted in some Hollywood movies. However, this is not true. Egyptian rulers compensated their citizens who worked on constructing the pyramids before the Abrahamic religions (Judaism, Christianity, and Islam) even existed. In fact, the pyramids were completed 900 years before the birth of Abraham, who is considered the patriarch of Judaism (Browder, 2007).

Q: Where did Africans go after leaving the continent of Africa?
A: Black Africans traveled across the globe. They were the first people to visit most parts of the world. Even in Europe, researchers now know that Black people were there 40,000 years ago, while

Modern humans began to exist approximately 200,000 years ago, and for about 90 percent of that time, the world was likely populated only by dark-skinned people.

they can only trace back the oldest genetic proof of modern white-skinned people to about 7,700 years ago (Eleftheriou-Smith, 2015). That means Black people have inhabited Europe for most of its existence. Africans were also the first to settle in India 50,000 years ago (Hays, 2017). Additionally, after leaving Africa, groups of hunter-gatherers inhabited an area that included Iran, southeastern Iraq, and northeastern Saudi Arabia for thousands of years. They then settled all of Asia and Europe about 45,000 years ago (Dunham, 2024). To be clear, despite the diverse populations in these areas today, the first settlers of these areas were Black Africans. Michael Petraglia, director of the Australian Research Centre for Human Evolution at Griffith University, describes the appearance of this area's early settlers:

The people inhabiting the hub at the time apparently had dark skin and dark hair, perhaps resembling the Gumuz or Anuak people now living in parts of East Africa" (Dunham, 2024).

Q: When did all humans cease to be dark-skinned people?
A: Famed paleoanthropologist Richard Leakey believes that the evidence to date suggests that for almost all of the existence of humanity, all humans were dark-skinned. It was not until very recently that the characteristics associated with White or Caucasian people began to exist. Modern humans began to exist approximately 200,000 years ago, and for about 90 percent of that time, the world was likely populated only by dark-skinned people (BBC News Africa, 2020).

Q: Okay, but what does all this African history have to do with me?
A: The European slave trade was the largest forced migration in human history and is the primary reason there are millions of Black people in North and South America today. Sadly, the schools that teach Black children in America too often start the story of Black life with slavery in the Americas. The period in which Europeans enslaved Africans, however, is minuscule compared to the length and depth of the totality of Black history. If a Black child starts the story of their history with slavery, they will never understand that their ancestors are the foundation of humanity. Without understanding how much Black people accomplished, one can never understand how much they lost when foreign slavers and colonizers uprooted their world.

Q: What part of Africa did most enslaved people in North and South America come from?
A: Most enslaved Africans in the Americas came from West and Central Africa. European slavers commonly took Africans from West Africa to the northern American colonies. European slavers tended to take the people they captured from Central Africa, however, to the southern American colonies (Holloway, 2005).

Q: What were West African empires like before Europeans invaded Africa?
A: Perhaps the three best-known West African empires are the successive empires of Ghana, Mali, and Songhai:

Ghana (300-1240)
Ghana was known as the land of gold. It became incredibly wealthy by controlling the trade of gold from Africans living south of Ghana and salt from those living north of Ghana. Laborers in Ghana retrieved gold from shallow mines or panned for gold nuggets and grains that would wash to the surface from rivers' floodwaters. Arab visitors noted that they could scoop up gold like sand in some areas (Mireille Harper, 2021). In addition to gold, merchants in Ghana also traded salt, daggers, silk, jewelry, timepieces, fine cloth, iron bars, leather, cotton, and kola nuts. At its peak, Ghana's population numbered in the millions and covered an area of 250,000 square miles. Tunka Menin (King in 1065) ruled with a court of counselors, ministers, interpreters, and treasurers. Menin maintained a standing army of 200,000 men, 40,000 of whom were archers (Karenga, 2002).

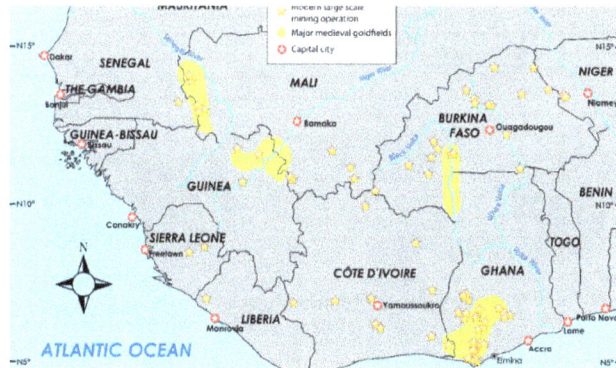
Fig. 7
Gold deposits in West Africa showing historical and modern mining activity.
Note. Source: (Garcia-Moreno, 2017).

Ghana's kings maintained their traditional religion, but as merchants and the ruling class developed relationships with Muslim traders, Islam took root in the empire and throughout the region. Ghana eventually collapsed after religious and cultural differences between Muslims and non-muslims weakened it. One point of contention between the two groups was Muslims' disapproval of the role of women in Ghana's traditional society. Women in Ghana had higher social, political, and economic status than women in other places, as they ran the markets and shaped the economy through their control of the pricing and distribution of products (Mireille Harper, 2021). Radical religious reformers' seizure of the capital city in 1076, along with prolonged droughts and more minor conflicts, led to Ghana's ultimate demise (Karenga, 2002).

Mali (1230-1468)

Mali developed out of a former Ghanaian state. Its first ruler was Sundiata Ali, but its most famous ruler was Mansa Musa (1312-1332). Musa built Mali into one of the world's largest empires. Musa extended Mali's borders and increased the empire's population to 10 million. Musa is perhaps best known for his legendary hajj in 1324. Some say on his 4,000-mile journey from West Africa to Mecca, he took 60,000 people and 80-100 camel loads of gold dust (Karenga, 2002). Musa's generosity had a negative impact on the economies of the regions he visited, as he freely distributed large amounts of gold, thereby reducing its scarcity and value there. Scholars consider Mansa Musa the wealthiest human in history, estimating his worth at $400 billion (Mulroy, 2022).

Fig. 8
1375 drawing of Mansa Musa.
Note. Source: (Cresques, 2023).

Furthermore, Musa arranged the construction of the University of Sankore at **Timbuktu**. The University of Sankore became a world-class intellectual center that attracted students and professors from around the world. Musa also encouraged the building of Quranic schools, which taught reading and writing to Mali's citizens. Kingdoms from as far away as France knew of Mansa Musa and his empire's wealth and power. Mali began to decline in 1400 and gave way to the next empire, Songhai, in 1468 (Karenga, 2002).

Songhai (1468-1591)

Songhai became the greatest of all West African empires. Under the leadership of Sunni Ali Ber, Songhai became the new power of West Africa in 1468. The empire solidified under Sunni Ali Ber's rule, though it was constantly at war. He drafted soldiers, organized a cavalry, and created a navy of war canoes to control the Niger River. Through his constant military conquests, Sunni Ali Ber enlarged the empire of Songhai. Songhai's most significant leader was Muhammad Toure, also known as "Askia the Great." Askia the Great built and governed an empire that stretched 2,000 miles long, making it almost as wide as the entire continent of Europe. He established and maintained many universities and schools that taught philosophy, medicine, law, government, astronomy, math, literature, ethnography, hygiene, logic, rhetoric, grammar, geography, music, and poetry writing. European, African, and Asian scholars visited Songhai to learn and exchange ideas. One professor, Ahmad Baba, is credited with writing 40 books ranging from astronomy to theology alone. After the death of Askia the Great, Songhai grew weaker due to poor leadership, and Moroccan invaders eventually conquered it in 1591 (Karenga, 2002).

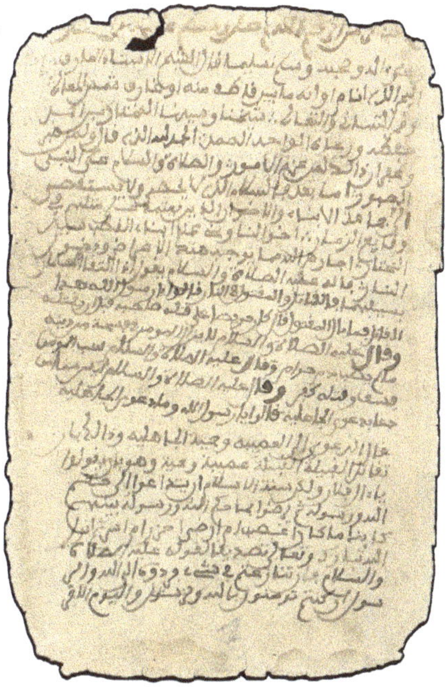

Q: Is it true that Africans did not have books, so they relied on oral storytellers for their history?
A: It is true that master oral historians, called griots, existed in Africa and could memorize and recite their people's history. However, while gold and salt were key industries in Songhai, books were the biggest industry in medieval West Africa. Leo Africanus wrote of the book trade in Songhai in 1526:

> There are in Timbuktu numerous judges, teachers and priests, all properly appointed by the king. He greatly honors learning. Many hand-written books imported from Barbary are also sold. There is more profit made from this commerce than from all other merchandise (Brians, 2016).

Fig. 9
A letter from a manuscript from Timbuktu.
Note. Source: (Library of Congress, 2014).

To this day, more than 700,000 books from this era are housed in Timbuktu, Mali, and thousands more are stored in private collections and institutions throughout West Africa (Walker, 2015). Some of the books were written in Arabic, which became a popular language for scholarly exchange among scholars and traders who shared ideas and knowledge. African scholars wrote other books in African languages or combinations of African languages and Arabic. Some of these West African writings date back to 800 A.D. (Walker, 2013). Google has digitized 40,000 of these African manuscripts online for public viewing (Google Arts & Culture Experiments, 2024).

Q: Before Europeans arrived, were West African societies just loose collections of straw and grass huts like I've seen on television?
A: Unlike the popular image of Africa in the Western media, West African societies were quite varied. Similar to Africa today, some people lived in more rural villages, but West African empires always had urban centers. The city of Timbuktu in the Mali Empire had a population of 100,000 people, including 25,000 students and scholars (The Editors of Encyclopedia Britannica, 2017). By comparison, medieval London's population was only about 20,000 (Walker, 2015).

Q: What was Europe like while these West African empires were flourishing?
A: Modern people would find medieval Europe a very difficult place to live. At the time of Columbus' voyage to the "New World," Europe was rife with diseases. Plagues, measles, influenza, diphtheria, typhus, typhoid fever, and smallpox killed Europeans by the thousands. Famine was common, and a fluctuation in the price of food could lead to thousands of people starving to death. Cities smelled horrible as European cities had ditches filled with stagnant water that citizens used as public toilets. Streets contained the decomposing bodies of dead animals and humans. The living people also were a source of foul smell, as most Europeans did not bathe regularly, and some never bathed in their entire lives. They also had rotting teeth and bad breath due to poor dental care, and it was common for Europeans to suffer from various skin diseases (Stannard, 1992).

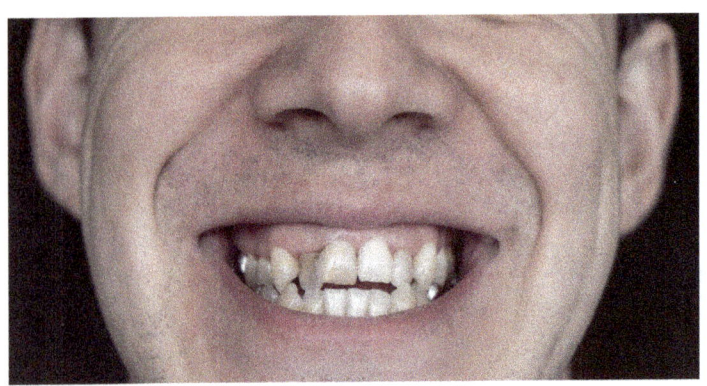
Fig. 10
Medieval Europeans commonly lacked dental care.
Note. Source: (anatolikFOTO, 2024).

Q: Yeah, but is it possible that everyone had the same health and hygiene challenges during this time?
A: While Europeans commonly threw human waste out of the windows of their homes into the street, the people of Songahi in West Africa had two-story homes with indoor plumbing systems where waste traveled down from second-story bathrooms to wells underneath the ground. People then poured hot water and pebbles down the toilet system to cover up offensive smells (School of Pan African Thought, 2016). At the same time, the average medieval European was filthy by modern

standards; in the 1500s, Africans in Songhai made and used soap and had books that described how to make toothpaste and how brushing could combat bad breath (Walker, 2013).

While Europeans commonly threw human waste out of the windows of their homes into the street, the people of Songhai in West Africa had two-story homes with indoor plumbing systems.

West Africans' deep understanding of medicine allowed them to live in a healthier environment than Europeans at the time. In the 1700s, Africans in Senegal, for instance, had a book of 2,000 to 3,000 known medicines, double the size of the Egyptians' record of medicines (Walker, 2013). While smallpox wreaked havoc on Europeans (who would later spread it to indigenous populations in the Americas), West Africans had been inoculating themselves against the disease for years. Many enslaved Africans were inoculated against smallpox before European slavers stole them from Africa (Walker, 2013). Africans from Senegal, Gambia, Guinea-Bissau, Guinea, Sierra Leone, Liberia, Côte d'Ivoire, Ghana, Togo, Benin, and parts of Nigeria-were all familiar with the practice of taking a small amount of pus from a smallpox patient and applying it to a small cut of a healthy person. That person would then become infected with a milder case of smallpox, which they could survive, resulting in the body producing antibodies that prevented future infections. One enslaved African in Boston, Onesimus, later taught the practice to his owner in the 1720s, who then spread the practice of smallpox inoculation throughout the American colonies (Mitchell, 2023).

Q: Are there any more African achievements people should know about?
A: We could write thousands of pages about the intellectual, cultural, economic, and spiritual accomplishments of Africans before foreign invaders permanently uprooted their world. The goal of our collection of African history highlights is to provide the reader with an understanding of how impressive African societies were before slavery and colonization. Too often, people possess the misconception that Africa was a largely unsettled and uncivilized place to which Europeans and others brought civilization. We hope we have established that this could not be further from the truth. Africa was the source of all that has sprung from humanity, and the brutal Trans-Atlantic and Trans-Saharan slave systems and Asian and European colonization interrupted the progress of the world's oldest people.

Lesson 2: Slavery

> ### Core Concepts
> - The Transatlantic Slave Trade was a system of racialized violence and economic exploitation created and dominated by Europeans, resulting in the forced migration and dehumanization of millions of Africans.
> - Slavery in the Americas was distinct for its brutality, lifelong chattel status, sexual violence, and deliberate destruction of African culture and identity.
> - Africans resisted at every stage, and understanding both their suffering and resistance is crucial to grasping the depth of slavery's impact on Black life today.

Language in the Lesson

Chattel slavery – A form of slavery where people are treated as permanent property.
Maafa – A Kiswahili word meaning "disaster" or "great tragedy," used to describe the total destruction caused by the slave system.
Middle Passage – The voyage across the Atlantic Ocean, where millions of Africans died in crowded ships.
Seasoning process – The process of violently "breaking in" newly enslaved Africans to plantation life.
Slave castles – Coastal fortresses in West Africa where enslaved Africans were imprisoned before shipment.

Q: What is the Transatlantic Slave Trade?
A: Even though we use the term "slave trade" in this text because readers are familiar with that term, historian Walter Rodney argues that the term "slave trade" conceals the system's atrocities by deflecting attention from its European perpetrators (Rodney, 1972). Some scholars argue that "trade" is too benign a term to capture the horrors of this system. Dr. Marimba Ani coined "**Maafa**" as a more accurate label. Maafa is a Kiswahili word that means disaster, terrible occurrence, or great tragedy. Ani explains that the term does not just describe the physical destruction of Black bodies but also the economic, cultural, spiritual, and psychological devastation that Europeans have inflicted on Black people across the world (Ani, 1994).

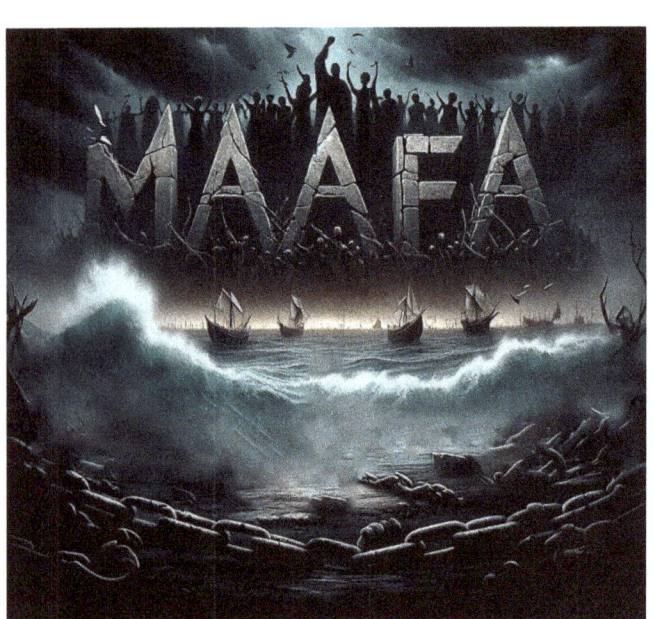

Q: When did Europeans begin to enslave Africans?
A: Historians know that the Portuguese were the first Europeans to enslave Africans. There are competing accounts of exactly when Portuguese sailors started taking African bodies out of West Africa. Some say they started in 1442 after visiting West Africa for gold the previous year, and when they returned to West Africa for more gold, they also brought 10 Africans back to Portugal (PBS, 2019). Other scholars say they cannot determine an exact year, but between 1441 and 1444, the Portuguese brought the first captured group of 240 West Africans to Portugal (Barragan, 2017).

The Portuguese made alliances with coastal African leaders and established trading posts and storehouses along the West African coast for the next several decades. They would go on to build 40 castles on the coast of West Africa, with the Elmina Castle (the oldest Portuguese outpost) and the Cape Coast Castle becoming the most well-known. The Portuguese initially built the castles as storage facilities for gold. However, they later repurposed them to serve as warehouses for enslaved Africans (PBS, 2019).

Q: Did Black people really help to enslave their own people in Africa?

A: Yes and no. Some Africans willingly captured and sold other Africans to European slave traders. In the grand scope of history, it is essential to remember that the idea of uniting around the color of one's skin is a recent concept. Africans did not view themselves as one people based on the color of their skin. Africans based their allegiances on the ethnic group and class to which they belonged, not on the color of one's skin. Thus, they were not concerned with the skin color of those they helped to enslave. Therefore, while it is true that Black people enslaved other Black people in Africa, Africans did not recognize the concept of a Black race that exists today (Antrim, 1999).

> *Africans did not view slavery as a permanent condition. Slavery in Africa ended after a set amount of years, and one's status as a slave was not passed from generation to generation.*

Q: Did Africans practice the same form of slavery as Europeans?

A: Africans' understanding of slavery was very different from that of Europeans. For instance, slaves amongst the Ashanti in West Africa could marry, own property, and own other slaves. Most importantly, Africans did not view slavery as a permanent condition. Slavery in Africa ended after a set amount of years, and one's status as a slave was not passed from generation to generation (PBS, 2019). Therefore, African groups that were politically and militarily strong, such as the Dahomey and Ashanti empires, had a history of selling captured rivals, enemies, the poor, and foreign groups even before European contact (Antrim, 1999). After several centuries of consistent conflict, like all of West Africa, the empires of these African slavers fell under the control of European countries, which became powerful from the profits they made off of the bodies and labor that enslaved Africans provided. The aftermath of Africans' collaboration with European slavers is seen today in places like Benin, where there is still a divide between some of the descendants of African slavers and the descendants of the people they enslaved (Sieff, 2018).

Q: Were all Africans who participated in the slave trade forced to do so?

A: No. It is a popular misconception that mighty Europeans swept into Africa and forced Africans into slavery. The truth is that African kingdoms were initially too strong and organized to be conquered by Europeans. Europeans did not have the military strength to force their will on Africa until the 1800s. Most European ships could not even reach the actual shores of West Africa because of hazardous offshore reefs and sandbars. Expert African sailors navigated canoes to the European ships and facilitated trade between Africans and Europeans docked a distance away. Additionally, Europeans' bodies were susceptible to diseases they could not counteract (Antrim, 1999). Africans willingly traded captured Africans to Europeans for luxury goods that were unavailable in Africa, not out of necessity. Africans were not dependent on European goods, but they became so when they began specializing in slaving at the expense of developing more diversified economies (Rodney, 1982).

Fig. 11
European Flintlock Musket from the 1700s.
Note. Source: (National Park Service, 2005).

Q: If Africa was independently wealthy, what did European merchants have to trade with Africans?
A: Europeans offered a variety of non-essential items to Africans in exchange for enslaved people. However, the most sought-after product was guns. Some estimates suggest that Europeans imported as many as 394,000 guns per year into Africa (Mustakeem, 2016). As more African rulers armed their soldiers with guns, their enemies had to do the same to protect themselves. It is important to note that these guns did not always function properly. One European trader admitted to dumping his broken and faulty guns on Africans, leading to frequent injuries as Africans lost fingers when the malfunctioning guns exploded (Mustakeem, 2016).

Q: So White people should be left off the hook for slavery, then?
A: The Transatlantic Slave Trade was entirely conceived and put into motion by Europeans, and they introduced levels of dehumanization, violence, and exploitation that Africans had never imagined. It was a European creation, and Europeans bear full responsibility for its consequences, regardless of any involvement from others. Throughout history, individuals have exploited their own communities for personal gain, as seen in instances such as African police officers enforcing apartheid laws in South Africa and Jewish police officers maintaining order for the Nazis in the Warsaw ghettos.

Distinguished professor of history, Black Studies, Gender Studies, and Women's Studies, Barbara Ransby, explains that though African elites did participate in capturing other Africans, Europeans created a new form of slavery based on race in which captured Africans and their offspring were enslaved for life. Race became the justification for the dehumanization and exploitation of Black bodies for three centuries. And even "free" Black people were deemed inferior just by virtue of physically looking like enslaved Black people. It is also critical to note that it was not the African elite who profited most from the enslavement of Africans. Europeans and Americans did not believe in profit-sharing, so they were primarily the beneficiaries of the wealth created from tobacco, sugar, cotton, and the millions of stolen hours of labor from enslaved Africans (Ransby, 2010).

Basil Davidson succinctly explained who was in charge of the Transatlantic Slave Trade:

> Africa and Europe were jointly involved [in the trade]. Yet it is also true that Europe dominated the connection, vastly enlarged the slave trade, and continually turned it to European advantage and to African loss (Davidson, 2004, p. 42).

Q: What were the phases of Africans' forced journey to the Americas?
A: Enslaved Africans' journey from their point of capture in Africa to the Western Hemisphere required them to endure three phases of suffering: 1) the death march, 2) slave castles, and finally, 3) slave ships that carried captured Africans across the Atlantic Ocean, sometimes referred to as the **Middle Passage**.

Q: What was the death march?
A: African slavers raided African villages at random times and kidnapped people to trade them to Europeans. By the 1700s, 70 percent of the captured Africans Europeans purchased were from kidnappings (Mustakeem, 2016). Slavers chained or tied captured Africans together, which limited their mobility and emphasized that they were no longer free. Once secured, slavers marched Africans from their point of capture to **slave castles** on the coast of West Africa, which could be up to 1,000 miles away. Africans who were too sick or tired to keep pace were often killed or left to die. Only about half of the captured Africans survived these marches (PBS, 2019b).

Fig. 12
Cape Coast Castle in Ghana
Note. Source: (Plummer, 2017).

Q: What were the conditions like in slave castles?

A: Once in the slave castles, Africans' captors warehoused them in underground dungeons until they packed them on ships. The dungeons within the fortresses, originally designed by Europeans to store non-living items like gold, had horrendous conditions. These rooms were extremely overcrowded, with hundreds of people in small, dark, hot, and poorly ventilated spaces where they had almost no room to move. The dungeons were disgusting. The overcrowded dungeons' lack of proper ventilation increased the likelihood of disease spread as slavers forced hundreds of captured Africans to live in their own urine and feces. This led to illness and diseases such as dysentery, malaria, and smallpox. European slavers cared little for the nourishment of the captured Africans, as they gave them just enough food to survive. In one instance, European slavers accidentally chose the wrong type of stone to grind the food that they served to captured Africans, which resulted in them ingesting mouthfuls of small stones, leading to multiple deaths (Smallwood, 2022).

Fig. 13
The dungeon floor for men at Cape Coast Castle in Ghana remains covered with inches of compacted human flesh, bones, and waste.
Note. Source: (Plummer, 2017).

Slavers regularly beat captured Africans and branded them with hot irons to mark them as property owned by someone else permanently (CNN, 2018). Women and girls' ordeal was particularly cruel as they were often victims of sexual violence from slavers. Slavers frequently raped captured African women and girls for pleasure and as a way of asserting their power over them (Jordan, 2007). Predictably, the slavers' physical, sexual, and psychological abuse of captured Africans led to high death rates. One historian estimates that 4 million captured Africans died before even reaching a slave ship (Manning, 2007).

Q: Once on the slave ships, why did Europeans make the conditions so horrible for captured Africans?

A: One of the functions of slave ships was to dehumanize Africans before they even began laboring as slaves in the Americas. Consequently, the crews on slave ships showed no compassion for captured Africans. European slavers viewed Africans as products simply to be bought and sold. Before slavers loaded captured Africans onto ships, they assigned numbers to them and separated them by sex. Slavers then performed insulting examinations of captured African girls and women by groping their breasts, buttocks, and vaginal areas as a so-called test of their childbearing ability. Slavers also molested African boys' and men's groins, scrotums, and anuses similar to the way a buyer examines a horse before purchase (Equal Justice Initiative, 2022).

On the ships, slavers intentionally tried to destroy Africans' identities by erasing captured Africans' names, languages, and cultural practices. They also separated captured Africans' families in an attempt to make them feel more isolated and helpless and less able to unite and rebel. Slavers frequently beat captured Africans with cat-o'-nine whips, which had multiple knotted cords that tore into flesh. Slavers sometimes punished captured Africans with thumbscrews that painfully crushed fingers, but otherwise left a person able to labor in the future. Slavers would force open the mouths of captured Africans engaged in hunger strikes using a speculum and pour food down their throats. Some slave ship captains tied Africans to their ships and towed them through the water as sharks devoured them to instill fear in the other captives. (Rediker, 2007).

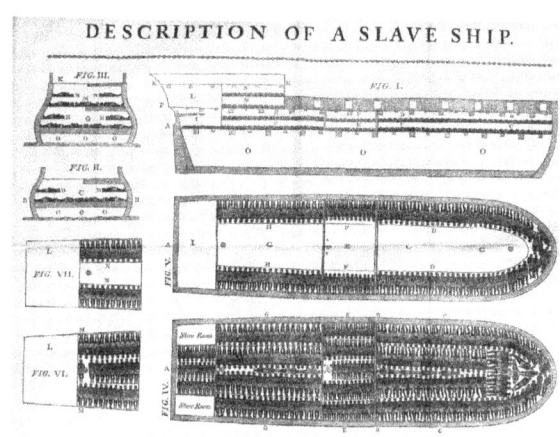

Fig. 14
1789 diagram of a slave ship that held slightly over 600 Africans captive.
Note. Source: (Phillips, 1789).

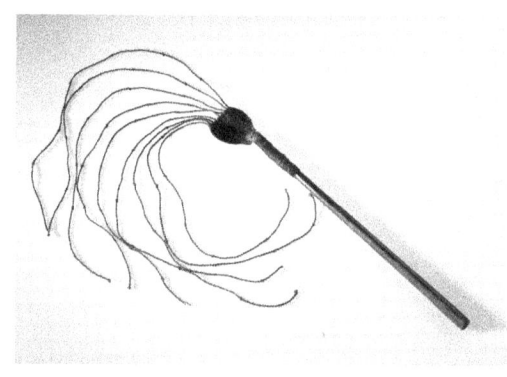

Fig. 15
A cat-o'-nine whip.
Note. Source: (Wellcome Images, 2014).

Along with the beatings and whippings, isolation, and forced feedings, women, men, and even both boys and girls were raped by slavers, further emphasizing that captured Africans were objects for slavers' pleasure and financial benefit (Anderson et al., 1995). On a ship in 1753, a slaver even publicly raped a pregnant captured African woman. Another slave ship captain raped a captured African girl between the ages of eight and ten for three nights in a row (Mustakeem, 2016). Slavers' depravity forced all captured Africans to deal with the daily psychological terror of seeing human beings tortured in unimaginable ways, with no understanding of when or if the abuse would ever stop.

When slavers did display an interest in preserving captured Africans' lives, they were not motivated out of sympathy but rather by the protection of eventual profit (Mustakeem, 2016).

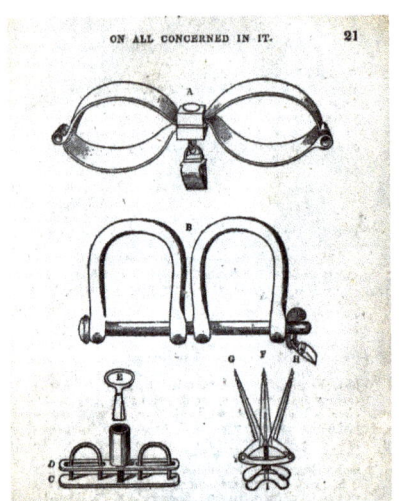

Fig. 16
Iron handcuffs, iron shackles, a thumb press, and a speculum oris. Note. Source: (Library Company of Philadelphia, 1836).

Q: Were captured Africans ever thrown overboard from ships as punishment?
A: Generally, slavers wanted to keep as many captured Africans alive and healthy as possible while simultaneously spending as little as possible to make that happen. Sometimes, though, slavers' view of captured Africans as property led to particularly horrific results. In 1781, the crew of the Zong overpacked the slave ship with 470 captured Africans. After weeks at sea, an outbreak of disease occurred. The ship's captain wanted to ensure a profit even if the captured Africans on board died. The ship's owner insured the voyage, but the insurance did not cover the costs of slaves who got sick or died from illness. The insurance did, however, cover slaves lost through drowning, so the captain decided he would throw overboard the slaves who did not look like they would recover from their illness. So, the captain ordered the crew to throw 54 captured Africans chained together overboard. Two days later, the captain ordered the crew to throw 78 more captured Africans overboard (Blight et al., 2019). Even though the captain did not own the ship, it was common for owners to give captains a percentage of whatever profit they made from the ship. Therefore, they were highly motivated to maximize profits from every journey, even if that meant relying on insurance payouts (Rediker, 2007).

Q: Did Africans fight back on slave ships?
A: Of course! Africans resisted during every phase of their enslavement. Records from slave ship crews show that fifteen percent of slave ship journeys were interrupted by direct revolts by captured Africans. Captured Africans carefully planned their revolts despite the language and cultural barriers they faced after European slavers chained them to strangers from unfamiliar places. Slave ship captains and their crews lived under constant threat of rebellion by captured Africans and had to find ways of discouraging it. After an unsuccessful rebellion on one slave ship, the captain wanted to kill two rebellion leaders as punishment. However, they were too valuable on the market to be

damaged. So, instead, the captain decided only to whip the two leaders, but delivered brutal public punishments to other Africans who were significantly less involved in the rebellion because they were less valuable on the market. The captain had one African man killed and made the surviving rebels eat his heart and liver. The captain then hanged an African woman who rebelled from her thumbs and then whipped and slashed her with knives until she died (Mustakeem, 2016)

Fig. 17
An artist's depiction of a slave ship revolt. Note. Source: (Trichon, 1883).

Despite slavers' public shows of violence designed to instill terror and fear into captured Africans, they continued to resist, as historians are aware of more than 500 slave ship rebellions. Other captured Africans revolted in non-violent ways. For example, captured Africans would sometimes engage in hunger strikes as a protest. To combat hunger strikes, slavers would use hot coals or a metal device called a speculum to force captured Africans to open their mouths and then pour food into them (Hine et al., 2014). Other captured Africans tried to throw themselves into the ocean rather than continue to be a part of the slavers' torturous system. The threat of slavers' lost profit from Africans jumping overboard became so common that slavers started attaching nets to the sides of ships to catch would-be jumpers (Hine et al., 2014).

Q: How were captured Africans from different backgrounds able to unite to resist enslavement?
A: The horrors of slave ships forced Africans from a variety of different geographic and cultural backgrounds to unite as one people to survive and execute revolts. These floating torture chambers became fertile grounds to plant seeds of what would later become African American culture (Rediker, 2007). Consequently, one could argue that the root of African American culture is resistance to violent White systemic racism.

Q: What were the effects of slavery on the African population that stayed on the continent?
A: The enslavement of Africans in the Americas had a profound impact on the continent of Africa. It led to a significant depopulation of the continent, resulting in the loss of an estimated 50-100 million

Even today, the most underdeveloped parts of Africa are where Europeans took the most people.

Africans. The depopulation of Africa represented a substantial depletion of human capital, expertise, and innovation, as many of the enslaved Africans were young and skilled individuals. The absence of these individuals hindered African societies' technological and cultural advancement (Karenga, 2002). Furthermore, the European slave trade disrupted and ultimately devastated previously diverse African economies. Even today, the most underdeveloped parts of Africa are where Europeans took the most people, and the average African income is almost five times lower than the rest of the world. One economist estimates that had foreigners not enslaved Africans, 72% of the average income gap between Africa and the rest of the world would not exist today (Nunn, 2017).

Fig. 18
Johann Moritz Rugendas' depiction of the public punishment of enslaved Black people in Brazil.
Note. Source: (Rugendas, 2020).

Q: Where did most enslaved Africans end up?

A: Brazil took the majority of enslaved Africans. This Portuguese-controlled colony received more enslaved Africans than any other country or territory in the Americas. From 1540 to the 1860s, of the 12.5 million enslaved Africans that slavers took to the Americas, 5.5 million were brought to Brazil (Princeton University, 2024). The effects of Brazil's prominent role in the slave trade are evident today, as 56% of the country is Black. The 120 million Afro-Brazilians in the country make it home to the largest Black population in the world outside of the African continent (Brito, 2022). The next largest recipients of enslaved Africans were islands in the Caribbean, followed by Spanish colonies in Latin America, and then finally the North American mainland. At one point, European-controlled territories profited from enslaved Africans from Canada down through Argentina. This explains the large number of Afro-Latinos that exist today. Because nearly 17% of enslaved Africans ended up in Spanish colonies, 25% of the people in Latin America today identify as Afro-Latinos (World Bank Group, 2023). It should be noted that what is now the United States only received approximately

3.6% of the enslaved African population from the Transatlantic Slave Trade (Slave Voyages Consortium, 2021).

Q: What made slavery in America different from previous forms of slavery?
A: American slavers forced enslaved Africans into a system of **chattel slavery**. Chattel slavery is different from other forms of slavery in that the enslaved people are considered property, not humans. Under chattel slavery, there is no difference between a human slave and a mule or a pig. As such, enslavers could subject enslaved people to incredibly inhumane living conditions, torture, and punishments without feeling they were committing crimes against humanity. Stephanie Smallwood says that slavers reduced Africans to "perishable commodities" (Yale University, 2020). A perishable commodity is a product that, by its nature, is subject to destruction, decay, deterioration, or spoilage (Law Insider, 2024). In other words, European slavers brought Africans with the understanding that they were merely disposable and replaceable items.

European slavers brought Africans with the understanding that they were merely disposable and replaceable items.

Q: What was the process of selling captured Africans to buyers in the Western world?
A: Once a ship anchored, slavers rowed captured Africans to the shore on small boats. Slavers would then line them up and march them to slave markets where anxious bidders would buy them (Stewart, 1996). Slave auctions were frequent events (six days a week in some places (McInnis et al., 2014) in public places where plantation owners, small farmers, and traders could bid on captured Africans. Captured Africans were held in pens before the auction started. Before buyers purchased anyone, they thoroughly examined captured Africans' bodies, checking their teeth, muscle tone, and number of scars, which were sometimes indicators that a captured African had a history of being punished for being rebellious. Slavers would wash captured Africans' bodies and cover their skin with grease, or sometimes tar (to cover scars and wounds), in an attempt to make them look healthy and thus more sellable (History on the Net, 2014). Auctioneers would then bring captured Africans onto a raised platform where the highest bidder would purchase each captured African presented for sale. W.L. Bost, who slavers held in bondage in North Carolina, describes a scene of an auctioneer selling a Black woman at a slave auction:

If they put up a young nigger woman, the auctioneer cry out: "Here's a young nigger wench, how much am I offered for her?" The poor thing stand on the block a-shivering and a-shaking nearly froze to death. When they sold, many of the poor mothers beg the speculators to sell them with their husbands, but the speculator only take what he want. So maybe the poor thing never see her husband again (Hurmence, p. 94, 1984/2005).

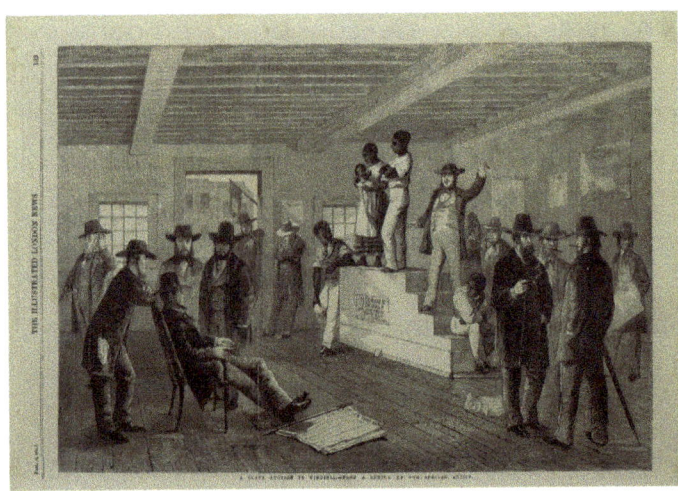

Fig. 19
1861 illustration of a Virginia slave auction
Note. Source: (Illustrated London News, 1861).

After the auctioneer sold their "merchandise," slaveowners took their newly acquired human property to their plantation, farm, or business. At that point, Africans transitioned from being captured to being enslaved as the permanent property of another person.

Q: After auctioneers sold enslaved Black people, how did they learn how to work in their new environments?
A: There was nothing about Africans' culture or biology that made them naturally fit to be slaves. Consequently, after being sold as property, no different from a wagon or a horse, enslaved Black people were forced to go through a *seasoning process* where slavers tried to undo all that they were so they could be efficient bonded workers. Slavers designed this period to break in newly purchased Black people. Slavers' goal was to break their spirit to resist and acclimate them to the expected routines and behavior. According to famed historian John Hope Franklin, the death rate among Black people going through a breaking-in process that lasted three to four years ran as high as 30 percent. "Old and new diseases, change of climate and food, exposure incurred in running away, suicide, and excessive flogging were among the main causes of the high mortality rates" (Franklin & Moss, 1998, p.45).

Q: Were there White slaves in America?
A: There were no White slaves in America. Europeans who were in debt or could not afford to pay for the trip to the American colonies could sell themselves into servitude for three to eleven years to pay the cost of the journey. These White laborers were indentured servants who worked alongside enslaved Africans and initially endured equally bad work and living conditions. The life of an

indentured servant was horrific enough for their average life span in the 1620s to be only about two years, so many died before becoming free. Consequently, enslaved Africans and White indentured servants complained, ran away, and rebelled together, most famously in the 1676 Bacon's Rebellion. This interracial rebellion among the poorest of workers terrified the wealthy, and they set out to divide enslaved Africans and White indentured servants against each other so they could never unite against the wealthy again (NPR, 2008).

To this end, the wealthy helped create the concept of Whiteness to separate bonded workers. The rich ensured that White servants were human, had a handful of rights, and their servitude was temporary, which made them feel superior to enslaved Africans, whom the wealthy gave no rights and relegated to mere property (NPR, 2008). Additionally, wealthy White people made Africans' condition of servitude permanent and passed it on to all of their offspring. Regardless of their place of origin, European indentured servants now became "White." White workers unified around their "Whiteness" instead of their economic and social interests, which were more aligned with those of enslaved Africans. Enslaved Africans, regardless of where they were originally from, now became Black slaves whom White servants viewed as inferior, even as they worked the same fields. Leslie Harris, a professor of history at Northwestern University, points out that indentured servitude is a contractual agreement between two people; slavery, however, is not a contract but more like being a prisoner of war (Stack, 2017).

Q: What types of horrors did enslaved Black people face in America?
A: Violence, terror, and abuse held the entire slave system together. Without having the legal sanction to punish and abuse enslaved Africans as they saw fit, slavers in America would not be able to hold the system together (Stampp, 1956). Maulana Karenga divides the types of torture Africans experienced into three categories: 1) physical, 2) sexual, and 3) psychological (2002).

Q: What are examples of the physical brutality enslaved Africans endured in America?
A: Physical abuse included whippings, beatings, mutilations, and malnutrition. The list of offenses that would move slaveholders to whip enslaved Black people included the most

> *Without having the legal sanction to punish and abuse enslaved Africans as they saw fit, slavers in America would not be able to hold the system together.*

trivial infractions. Enslaved Black people were liable to be whipped if they looked dissatisfied, looked too proud, spoke too loudly, forgot to take off their hat when approaching a White person, broke a plow or hoe, or failed to show enough respect to White people (Douglass, 1845).

Kenneth Stamp explained how slavers determined the number of whip lashes they would give as punishment. If the whip consisted of a leather strap, 15 to 20 lashes were sufficient to discipline most slaves. Slaveholders would allow more lashes in some extreme cases, but were sometimes merciful enough to limit the whippings to a maximum of 100 lashes per day. Enslaved Black people would receive fewer lashes when slavers used the "rawhide" whip. The rawhide whip was made of about three feet of ox hide and was an inch thick at its end. It was a "savage instrument requiring only a few strokes to provide a chastisement that a slave would not soon forget" (Stampp, 1956, p.176).

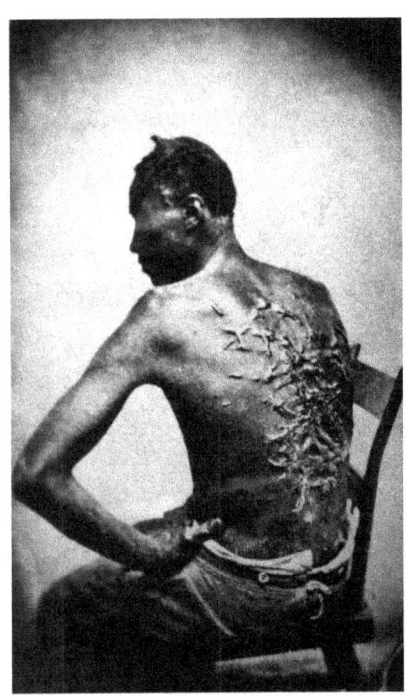

Fig. 20
1863 photograph of "Whipped Peter."
Note. Source: (Brady, 1863.

Slavers found other ways to punish enslaved Black people besides whippings. They would make enslaved Black people who "misbehaved" serve other people food without being allowed to eat any themselves, put enslaved Black people in solitary confinement in plantation jails, and place others in stocks for a week. Slavers even forced enslaved Black people to eat any worms they failed to pick off tobacco leaves (Stampp, 1956). In some cases, slavers punished enslaved Black people who rebelled by cutting off their ears, pulling out their teeth, or cutting off their hands if they were caught in the act of attacking a White person (Turnbull, 2020). Other brutal plantation punishments slavers inflicted on enslaved Africans included the denial of food and shelter, branding, pouring salt into open wounds, allowing dogs to maul runaways, boiling them alive, skinning them alive, and burying them alive (Karenga, 2002).

Q: What are examples of the sexual brutality enslaved Africans endured in America?
A: Sexual brutality usually took the form of rape and "breeding." Breeding was the practice of slavers forcing their largest and strongest enslaved Africans to have sex in the hopes of creating physically superior offspring who would become valuable workers or profitable products on the slave

market. Breeding was a common practice, and the thought process behind it resembled that of animal breeders. Daina Ramey Berry points out that newspaper articles' descriptions of the slave breeders' system sounded eerily similar to articles on animal husbandry. Articles like "How to Raise a Negro," explained the process of breeding Black workers in a way that matched other articles about breeding pigs (Not Even Past, 2011). The sexual abuse that slavers inflicted on enslaved Black people was a form of psychological as well as physical abuse. Enslaved Black families had to endure the pain and humiliation of slavers forcing them to have sex with people other than their spouses or partners to create more people for profit (Berry, 2011). Slavers' sexual abuse of enslaved Black people was a constant reminder that everything belonged to their White slavers, even their own bodies.

> *Slavers' sexual abuse of enslaved Black people was a constant reminder that everything belonged to their White slavers, even their own bodies.*

Q: What are examples of the psychological brutality enslaved Africans endured in America?
A: Talmadge Anderson argues that one cannot even begin to understand the slave system and its effect on Black people without seeing it as an oppressive form of physical and psychological torture of enslaved Black people's minds, bodies, and souls. Enslaved Black people were constantly subjected to torture, similar to what prisoners of war have suffered:

> They were tortured to force the revelation of information of revolts and to incriminate and betray fellow slaves. Torture was used to indoctrinate the slave with the values and wishes of the slaveholders to force the abandonment of their African beliefs and practices. Torture and beating were standard methods of intimidation employed for the purpose of deterring rebellion and evoking a spirit of docility. Isolation was a form of torture in itself. Unapproved and unwarranted congregating were met with punishment (Anderson, 1993, p. 168).

Maulana Karenga describes slavers' psychological brutality as the "daily humiliation, denial and deformation of African history and humanity" (Karenga, 2002, p. 142). The list of psychologically damaging events that enslaved Africans lived through is almost endless. Enslaved Africans had to deal with the terror caused by slaveholders and their employees raping their loved ones. They also lived under the constant threat of slavers selling their family members away from them.

Slavers' attempts to teach enslaved Africans that they were biologically and culturally inferior to White people and should always be submissive to them amount to cultural genocide:

> By cultural genocide is meant, the wholesale intentional destruction of a people's culture and cultural identity and their capacity to produce, reproduce and expand themselves. It includes the destruction of: 1) political identities and ethnic units and identities; 2) families; and 3) cultural leaders. These were all units of the preservation and transmission of African culture. But they were also units of real and potential resistance — on the cultural and physical level and thus, the enslaver sought to destroy them (Karenga, 2002, p. 143).

The systematic erasure of African identity by slavers has devastating effects on Black people in America to this day. This is why many African Americans must rely on scientists to trace their ancestry by analyzing their DNA and comparing it to that of individuals with similar traits throughout the diaspora. The erasure of enslaved Black people's language, culture, and belief systems is why Black people in the Americas have European names and must use the language of their oppressors (e.g., English, Spanish, Portuguese, French, etc.) to communicate.

Q: What was a day like for an enslaved Black person?
A: The whippings and other cruel punishments that enslaved Black people received were in addition to the inhumane conditions they labored under. Former slave Solomon Northup describes a typical day in the life of an enslaved Black person on a cotton plantation:

> The hands are required to be in the cotton field as soon as it is light in the morning, and, with the exception of ten or fifteen minutes, which is given them at noon to swallow their allowance of cold bacon, they are not permitted to be a moment idle until it is too dark to see, and when the moon is full, they often times labor till the middle of the night. They do not dare to stop even at dinner time, nor return to the quarters, however late it be until the order to halt is given by the driver (1853/2009).

After the workday was over, enslaved Black people had to carry the cotton they picked to the gin-house to be weighed. Enslaved Black people faced this routine with fear. Those whose baskets of cotton fell short of the daily quota knew they would be whipped as punishment (Northup, 1853/2009). If they exceeded slave drivers' expectations, they would be expected to overachieve every day.

It was an entirely no-win situation for enslaved Black people. Even after the daily cotton weighing and the subsequent whippings, the work day was not over. Enslaved Black people still had to do chores in their quarters, such as feeding mules and pigs, cutting wood, kindling fire, grinding corn with a small hand mill, and preparing meals for the next day. When enslaved Black people completed all these chores, they were finally able to retire, only to be awakened an hour before daylight by the sound of the overseer's horn the next day (Northup, 1853/2009).

A WOMAN WITH IRON HORNS AND BELLS ON, TO KEEP HER FROM RUNNING AWAY.

Fig. 21
Note. Source: (Schomburg Center for Research in Black Culture, Manuscripts, Archives and Rare Books Division, The New York Public Library, 1839).

Some states were worried that overworking enslaved Black people could lead to rebellions, so they limited their work to only 15 hours per day (Franklin & Moss, 1998). On George Washington's slave plantation in Mount Vernon, Virginia, enslaved Black people worked about 8 hours a day in the winter when the days were shorter. During the summer, they could work up to fourteen hours daily (Mount Vernon Ladies' Association, 2024).

Q: Was it easier to be an enslaved Black woman than a man?
A: Absolutely not. Slavers expected enslaved Black women to do the same amount of work as enslaved Black men. Even when pregnant, slavers expected enslaved Black women to work full days until childbirth (Hine et al., 2014) and whipped them when they could not keep pace with everyone else working. Slavers even whipped enslaved pregnant women who stopped working to care for their infants with a cart whip as punishment for wasting time (Franklin & Moss, 1998). Enslaved Black women also bore the burden of frequent sexual abuse and violence. Enslaved Black women were property in this system and, as such, had no rights to their own bodies. Consequently, enslaved Black women had to do a full day's work while also dealing with slavers who raped them, impregnated them, and forced them to bear children for profit. Even when enslaved Black women birthed slavers' children, slavers did not guarantee they or their children would be treated any kinder (Matthews & Florida State College at Jacksonville, 2021).

Slavers even whipped enslaved pregnant women who stopped working to care for their infants with a cart whip as punishment for wasting time.

Although it was not as common an occurrence as White men raping enslaved Black women, enslaved Black women were also sometimes raped by enslaved Black men. State law, however, generally did not consider Black women worthy of protection from rape. A Tennessee judge sentenced an enslaved Black man to death for raping a White woman but added that if the victim had been Black, the attacker would not have broken any law. A Mississippi law only defined an enslaved Black man raping an enslaved Black female as a crime if she was under the age of twelve (White, 1999). Sadly, this double burden of Black women having to fight for freedom, security, and prosperity both inside and outside of the Black community became a part of Black life in America that still exists to this day.

Enslaved Black women were very aware of their horrific predicament. Harriet Jacobs, in her slave narrative, *Incidents in the Life of a Slave Girl*, wrote about her frequent resistance to sexual advances from slavers. Once, while hiding for safety, the despair she felt was so deep that she considered killing her own child rather than letting her live through the same horrible experiences she had in slavery (Jacobs & Douglass, 2011).

Women, of course, resisted sexual exploitation in any way they could, even if it cost them their lives. In 1885, a 19-year-old enslaved Black woman named Ceila grew tired of being repeatedly raped by the slaver who owned her, so she fought back by fatally hitting him in the head with a club. Though the slaver had raped her from ages 14 to 19, the White community called for her punishment. Ceila went on trial, and after ten days, the court convicted her and ordered her to be hanged for killing her rapist and slaver (Matthews & Florida State College at Jacksonville, 2021).

Q: It is common knowledge that White men had sex with enslaved Black people. Did White women do the same?
A: Yes. Though not mentioned often, just like White men, White women had sex with enslaved Black people. In T*he Slave Community*, John Blassingame references court records that show White men suing for divorce from their White wives because of their infidelity with enslaved Black men (1979).

Q: Were White women nicer to enslaved people than their husbands
A: Too often, only White men are cast as the slave system's wrongdoers while White women are silent bystanders. While there are incidents of White women being kinder to enslaved Black people

than their husbands (such as the White woman who taught Frederick Douglass to read), enslaved Black people also recall White women being violently racist towards them. In a 1937 interview, former slave Ria Sorrell gave her impression of her "master," Jacob Sorrell, versus his wife:

> There was about twenty-five slaves on the place, and Marster just wouldn't sell a slave. When he whupped one, he didn't whup much; he was a good man. He seemed to be sorry every time he had to whup any of the slaves. His wife was a pure devil; she just joyed whupping Negroes (Hurmence, 1984/2005, p. 63).

Sorrel stated that the master's wife whipped slaves as often as she could when he was away. She also regularly denied food to enslaved Black people or provided them with inferior quality food, but the master would supply better quality food to the enslaved people he owned without his wife's knowledge. However, Sorrel mentioned that the couple did agree on one thing:

> There is one thing they wouldn't allow, and that was books and papers. I can't read and write (Hurmence, 1984/2005, p. 64).

Q: Why were slavers so against enslaved Black people learning to read and write?

A: During slavery, some states felt it necessary to ban teaching slaves to read and write legally. Some Southerners viewed a literate slave population as rebellious and dangerous, and thus, they saw the teaching of enslaved Black people as a criminal act. In his classic work, *The Narrative of the Life of Frederick Douglass*, Frederick Douglass gave a clear example of how important it was for slave owners to hold their "property" in a state of ignorance. The wife of Frederick Douglass' enslaver began to teach him how to read, but her husband cut his learning short when he discovered it:

> ...Mr. Auld found out what was going on and at once forbade Mrs. Auld to instruct me further, telling her, among other things, that it was unlawful, as well as unsafe, to teach a slave to read. To use his own words further, he said, "If you give a nigger an inch, he will take an ell. A nigger should know nothing but to obey his master to do as he is told to do. Learning would spoil the best nigger in the world. Now," said he "if you teach that nigger (speaking of myself) how to read, there would be no keeping him. It would forever unfit him to be a slave. He would at once become unmanageable and of no value to his master. As to himself, it could do him no good but a great deal of harm. It would make him discontented and unhappy (Gates, 1987, pp. 274-275).

Illiteracy was a powerful weapon in slavers' fight to control the behavior of enslaved Black people. By denying enslaved Black people the ability to read, slavers stifled their ability to discover any alternatives to their current lives. Slavers' fears were not unfounded, as enslaved Black people who could read and write were active in slave rebellions in both the 1700s and 1800s (Walker, 1992). Some states, like Virginia in 1831, even passed laws that made it illegal for Virginians to teach free Black people to read and write (Encyclopedia Virginia, 2020).

Q: What did it mean to be "sold down the river?
A: The United States banned the importation of new enslaved Africans from overseas after 1808. However, this did not decrease the demand for Black slave labor among White slavers. A new domestic slave trade emerged, wherein slavers purchased the enslaved Black workers they needed from various regions within the United States. Slavers and breeders, as they saw fit, sold enslaved Black people away from their families for profit. This led to slavers ripping 1.2 million enslaved Black people from their families as they were sold and transported across the country. Enslaved Black families lived in dread of slavers selling their loved ones "down the river" deeper into the South, to places like Louisiana sugar plantations that had deadly reputations. Interestingly, after the United States banned the importation of new enslaved Africans from overseas, the enslaved population of Black people tripled (Mintz, 2019).

Fig. 22
Harpers Weekly's illustration of enslaved Black people operating a cotton gin.
Note. Source: (Sheppard, 2017).

Q: How did the invention of the cotton gin change life for enslaved Black people?
A: The cotton gin is a machine that quickly separates cotton fibers from seeds. This invention significantly increased the speed at which cotton could be prepared for sale. Cotton producers wanted as much raw cotton as they could get their hands on, as it was like being able to grow money from the ground. Consequently, slavers aggressively and violently increased the workload for enslaved Black people picking raw cotton. It was common for slavers to expect enslaved Black people (both men and women) to pick 100 to 200 pounds of cotton per day. Enslaved Black people's speedy work under the threat of being whipped one

time for each pound under their daily quota drove almost every other cotton-producing country out of business. The South produced 1.4 million pounds of cotton in 1800, but by 1860, enslaved Black people had harvested 2.5 billion pounds in a single year. Of the cotton that enslaved Black people harvested, 80% was exported overseas, with most of it going to Britain (Baptist, 2015).

It was common for slavers to expect enslaved Black people (both men and women) to pick 100 to 200 pounds of cotton per day.

Q: So, was death the only escape from the American chattel slave system?
A: Even after death, slavers would harvest enslaved Black people's bodies for profit. Daina Ramey Berry says that there was another slave trade, which she calls the domestic cadaver trade, that involved selling dead Black bodies to medical schools. Slavers found out they could sell deceased Black people for five to thirty dollars to representatives from medical schools that would then use them as part of anatomical dissection and research for human anatomy courses. Some of these medical colleges would use enslaved Black people as grave robbers to procure cadavers (Berry, 2018).

Free Black people faced the same issue with their dead loved ones. While enslaved Black people had limited options in how to bury and protect their dead, some free Black people would try to thwart grave robbers by sealing their loved ones' caskets, burying them with bells so they could hear if grave robbers attempted to move their bodies, or by employing night watchmen to patrol graveyards (Berry, 2018).

Q: How many free Black people were there during American slavery?
A: Historian Ira Berlin says that shortly before the start of the American Civil War, there were about half a million free blacks in America, with a slight majority of them living in the South. Free Black people in the North and South both had their legal rights limited. In the North, White people banned them from the best jobs, so they had to work as domestics and laborers. In most places, free Black people in the North could not run for political offices, sit on juries, testify against Whites, or be a part of a militia. They could, however, form Black clubs, organizations, and churches, which led to the creation of a Black leadership class. Free Black people in the South made more money than their Northern counterparts, but their lives were more regulated as they had limits on where they could

travel and had to carry passes designating them as free. Free Blacks lived on the fringes of Southern society as slavers saw their existence as a bad example for enslaved Black people and an unsettling preview of what the future could look like (Berlin & WGBH Educational Foundation, 2024). Therefore, despite whatever success free Black people in the South enjoyed, Berlin points out that even the lowest of Whites could threaten free Black people "with a good nigger beating" (Gates, Jr., 2013).

Q: Did enslaved Black people ever fight back while they were on plantations?
A: Just as they did on slave ships, enslaved Black people constantly resisted their oppression in both small and large ways. Enslaved Black people resisted through work slowdowns, labor strikes, pretending to be sick or hurt, intentionally breaking tools, stealing property, poisoning slavers' and their families' food, and running away (Karenga, 2002).

Because enslaved Black women often served as cooks on slave plantations, they were able to use their position to poison slavers and their families.

As they had been on slave ships, women were central to enslaved Black people's resistance against slavery. One tool of resistance that was readily available to enslaved Black women was poison. Because enslaved Black women often served as cooks on slave plantations, they were able to use their position to poison slavers and their families. The White community in Charleston, South Carolina, burned a Black woman alive in 1755 for poisoning her slaver. In 1769, a South Carolina newspaper ran an article about Mary Churchill, who poisoned her slaver and his infant. When Churchill's slaver accurately accused her of poisoning him over several months, she did not wait to find out what her punishment would be. Instead, she and two enslaved Black men cut their slaver's throat in the middle of the night and then ran away (White, 1999).

As far as full-scale revolts, Herbert Aptheker identified 250 rebellions from the American colonial period through the Civil War (Aptheker, 2013). Arguably, the most famous rebellion was that organized by Nat Turner in 1831 in Virginia. Turner led more than 50 enslaved Black freedom fighters in a bloody revolt in Southampton, Virginia, killing almost 60 White people, including women and children. The local authorities were able to stop the rebellion by the next day and killed most of the rebels, though Turner eluded them for sixty days (Allyn, 2024).

As punishment for Turner's rebellion, White mobs killed up to 200 Black people who had no involvement with Turner's rebellion. As for Turner, several reports say that after White mobs hanged Turner, they gave his dead body to doctors for dissection, who then shared his body parts with several White families. One writer recorded that "Turner was skinned to supply such souvenirs as purses, his flesh made into grease, and his bones divided as trophies to be handed down as heirlooms" (Klein, 2016).

Other revolts that shook the slave-owning community include the Stono Rebellion in South Carolina (1739), Gabriel Prosser's Rebellion in Virginia (1800), the German Coast Uprising in Louisiana (1811), and Denmark Vesey's Conspiracy in South Carolina (1822).

Q: How did enslaved Black people's belief systems and culture help them survive chattel slavery?
A: Enslaved Black people's minds were their greatest tool in the struggle to survive chattel slavery. John Blassingame's work shows that enslaved Black people's preservation of African music, dance, folklore, and religious practices while incorporating new ideas from America created a unique African American culture separate from that of their White slavers, which provided psychological strength and a sense of community that allowed them to survive (Blassingame, 1972).

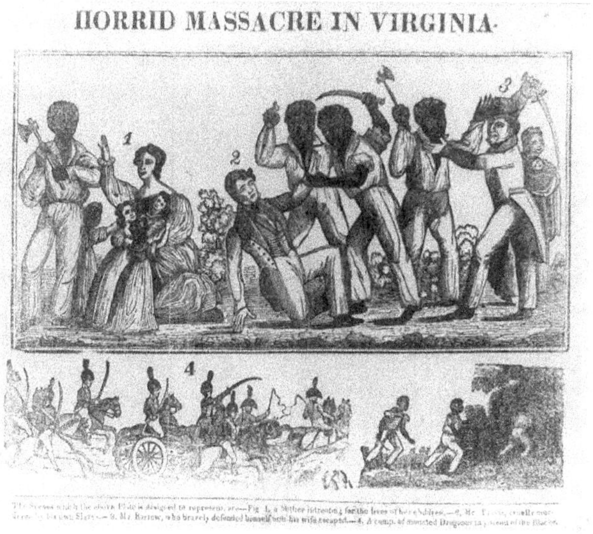

Fig. 23
An illustration of Nat Turner's rebellion.
Note. Source: (Authentic and Impartial Narrative of the Tragical Scene Which Was Witnessed in Southampton County, 2007).

Q: Is it true that some Black people in America owned slaves?
A: Indeed, some free Black people in the South owned Black people and, at times, treated them harshly, just like White slavers did. These Black slave owners typically included freed children of White slavers, Black people who had fought in military conflicts, or those who had bought their own freedom. Various factors contributed to why these Black individuals enslaved others. As free Black business owners in the South thrived, their demand for

workers grew. Often, White workers were unwilling to take jobs with Black employers, leading to their reliance on enslaved Black people as the available labor pool. Some free Black people bought family members to prevent them from being sold away by White slavers. Additionally, other Black slave owners viewed the ownership of enslaved individuals as a cultural and economic standard among successful people in the South and thus felt justified in participating in the dehumanization of fellow Black people for profit and social standing. (Koger, 1985).

Q: Did any U.S. Presidents own slaves?
A: George Washington, the first President of the United States, was a wealthy slaver in Virginia. At various times, George Washington wore dentures made of metal or ivory, but also from the teeth of some of the Black people he enslaved. Washington never rejected the American slave system and never freed any of the Black people he enslaved while he lived (Kimberley, 2020). Washington continuously viewed enslaved Black people as lesser objects that were often a nuisance. Washington made his stepson go to college in New York instead of Virginia because Washington hoped that being in New York would tame his child's unacceptable behavior, which included gambling and having sex with enslaved Black people (Wilder, 2014). Ironically, 90 percent of Americans with the last name Washington today are Black (Franke-Ruta, 2011).

Fig. 24.
1851 painting of George Washington at Mount Vernon, depicting enslaved Black people working on his farm.
Note. Source: (Stearns, 2019).

Washington's participation in American chattel slavery was not unique among American Presidents. The men who held the Presidency for 32 of the first 36 years of America's existence were slaveholders from Virginia: George Washington, James Monroe, Thomas Jefferson, and James Madison (Morgan, 1975). Additionally, only two of the first 12 Presidents of the United States were not slavers at some point in their lives. The complete list of U.S. Presidents who owned slaves is:

George Washington (1st President)
Thomas Jefferson (3rd President)
James Madison (4th President)
James Monroe (5th President)
Andrew Jackson (7th President)
Martin Van Buren (8th President

William Henry Harrison (9th President)
John Tyler (10th President)
James K. Polk (11th President)
Zachary Taylor (12th President)
Andrew Johnson (17th President)
Ulysses S. Grant (18th President)

Q: But wasn't slavery just one of many big businesses in America?

A: Slavery was *the* business of America. Historian Edward Baptiste's work explains the dominance of slavery in the American economy:

> The bodies of the enslaved served as America's largest financial asset, and they were forced to maintain America's most exported commodity. In 60 years, from 1801 to 1862, the amount of cotton picked daily by an enslaved person increased 400 percent. The profits from cotton propelled the U.S. into a position as one of the leading economies in the world and made the South its most prosperous region. The ownership of enslaved people increased wealth for Southern planters so much that by the dawn of the Civil War, the Mississippi River Valley had more millionaires per capita than any other region (Lockhart, 2019).

Q: What colleges profited from slavery in America?

A: Chattel slavery and education existed together in America's oldest schools. The country's first public school, Boston Latin, founded in 1635, had enslaved Black people working its grounds (Mor et al., 2023). Not surprisingly, many of America's oldest schools of higher learning also profited from chattel slavery by accepting money from slavers, owning and selling enslaved Black people, using enslaved Black people to build their campuses, using enslaved Black people for labor on campus, investing in industries fueled by enslaved Black people's labor, or even charging students extra money to bring their enslaved Black laborers with them to college (Wilder, 2014). The following is a

Fig. 25.
Flags from several Ivy League schools
Note. Source: (Zirkel, 2018).

partial list of schools that recognize their direct connection to chattel slavery:

- Harvard University (Wilder, 2014)
- William & Mary University (William & Mary, 2024)
- Yale University (Reid, 2024)
- Massachusetts Institute of Technology (Wilder et al., 2020)
- Brown University (Brown University, 2021)
- Dartmouth College (Dartmouth & Slavery Project, 2024)
- Columbia University (Columbia University, 2014)
- Princeton University (Sandweiss & Hollander, 2024)
- Rutgers University (Scarlet and Black Research Center, 2024)
- Washington University in St. Louis (WashU & Slavery Project, 2024)
- University of Pennsylvania (Department of History, University of Pennsylvania, 2022)
- Georgetown University (Georgetown University, 2024)
- Clemson University (Riddle, 2015)
- University of South Carolina (Horn, 2017)
- Wake Forest University (Wake Forest University Slavery, Race and Memory Project, 2024)
- Johns Hopkins University (Schuessler, 2020)
- University of Alabama (Buckley et al., 2024)
- University of Virginia (University of Virginia Library, 2016)
- University of North Carolina at Chapel Hill (Fortin, 2018)
- University of Maryland (Price, 2024)
- Emory University (King, 2024)
- Vanderbilt University (Miao, 2021)
- University of Georgia (Hebbard, 2022)
- Tulane University (Axelrod & Faulkner, 2019)
- University of Mississippi (University of Mississippi Graduate School, 2020)

Currently, a group of educational institutions in the United States, Canada, and Europe is known as Universities Studying Slavery (USS). This consortium is dedicated to thoroughly researching and documenting their institutions' historical ties to chattel slavery (University of Virginia Library, 2016).

Q: Who profited from the Trans-Atlantic slave trade other than slave owners themselves?
A: The list of those who profited from the enslavement of Black people is extensive and far-reaching, including the following:

Religious Institutions

Massive religious institutions like the Church of England and the Roman Catholic Church both directly profited from slavery. The Church of England's endowment fund is worth over $12 billion. Part of the fund's success is due to the church's willingness to invest in the Transatlantic Slave Trade during the 18th century (Lawless, 2023). The Roman Catholic Church sanctioned the slave business and received payment to settle disputes between European nations fighting over territory to enslave and colonize (Anderson, 1995). Factions of the Catholic Church also owned slaves, such as the Jesuits, who owned over 20,000 enslaved people in 1760 (Kellerman, 2023). When Georgetown University was on the verge of bankruptcy, the Jesuits sold 272 of the Black people they enslaved to prevent the school from going under and to help stabilize the Jesuits in Maryland (Swarns, 20).

Fig. 26
St. Peter's Square in Vatican City.
Note. Source: (Diliff, 2007).

Fig. 27
Lloyd's of London Building
Note. Source: (Lloyd's of London, 2015).

Insurance Companies

Several existing insurance companies received huge financial boosts by helping to enslave Black people. Lloyds of London transitioned from a coffee house to the largest insurance marketplace by insuring slave ships and their human cargo (Anderson, 1995). New York Life, Aetna, and AIG also sold insurance policies that covered the Black people held captive by slavers (Morain, 2002).

Banking and Finance

Banks made money from chattel slavery through loans to slavers and accepted enslaved Black people as property that borrowers could use as collateral. American banks that acknowledged their connection to chattel slavery include J.P. Morgan Chase, Citibank, Bank of America, and Wells Fargo (Thomas, 2019).

Banks in the United Kingdom that profited from slavery include the Royal Bank of Scotland, Barclays Bank, HSBC, Lloyds Banking Group, and Arbuthnot Latham (Jolly, 2020). The Bank of England also released a report detailing its ownership of 599 slaves and its role in providing mortgages for plantations (Jolly, 2022).

Clothing Companies

Present-day high-end suit retailer Brooks Brothers has clothed 40 U.S. presidents (Maryland Center for History and Culture, 2020). But its success is at least partially based on the servant clothing it manufactured and sold to slavers who wanted formal wear for their enslaved Black servants:

> The ready-made suit was a turning point for the garment industry and for the American population, making fine clothing more accessible to all,' wrote the company recently in its online magazine. What has not been examined is how much this innovation might have been based on its outfitting of free and enslaved servants who did not have the time or luxury to be fitted for bespoke garments (Michael, 2021).

The labor of enslaved Black people played a crucial role in the supply chain for lower-end clothing, too, paving the way for the production of Levi Strauss jeans and other denim brands. Slavers exploited the knowledge that these individuals brought from West Africa, particularly in extracting blue dye from indigo, to cultivate it alongside cotton on plantations. Notably, due to the durability of denim, slavers provided this fabric for enslaved Black workers to wear during their laborious tasks (Bicks & Strachan, 2022). Tragically, enslaved Black people ultimately wore the very products of their own relentless toil.

Fig. 28
A CSX locomotive.
Note. Source: (Levisay, 2014).

Sugar

Domino's Sugar became incredibly wealthy by selling "white gold," which was harvested by enslaved Black people enduring backbreaking labor on plantations. Due to the intense work required for constant sugar harvesting, the life expectancy of enslaved Black people on a sugar plantation was only about seven years (Muhammad, 2019).

Railroads

North America's major present-day rail companies, CSX, Norfolk Southern, Pacific Union, and Canadian National, all own rail lines that were constructed by enslaved Black people (Cox, 2002). In places like North Carolina, rail companies forced enslaved Black people (both men and women) to dig track beds, lay tracks, and serve as cleaners, brakemen, maintenance workers, and cooks (National Park Service, 2022). Nearly every Southern railroad before the Civil War was built by the labor of enslaved Black people, including rail construction ordered by the U.S. Military Railroads (USMRR) (National Park Service, 2023).

Federal Government Projects

Two of the biggest U.S. federal government projects involving enslaved Black people were the White House and the Capitol Building. Enslaved Black people contributed to every stage of the construction of the White House, and they helped rebuild it after the British burned it down in 1814. Presidents Thomas Jefferson, James Madison, James Monroe, John Quincy Adams, Andrew Jackson, Martin Van Buren, John Tyler, James K. Polk, and Zachary Taylor all either brought enslaved Black people with them or hired them out to work at the White House (White House Historical Association, 2024).

The government leased enslaved Black people from slavers in Virginia and Maryland so that they could have a cheap labor force while technically not owning any slaves. The leased enslaved Black people worked the quarries where they excavated the sandstone needed for the Capitol Building. They also cleared the trees from the wooded area where workers would eventually build the Capitol Building. After clearing the area, enslaved Black people performed various tasks, including carpentry, masonry, rafting, plastering, brick making, sawing, and painting for the building. They did this backbreaking work six days a week without pay or recognition (Fling, 2024).

Fig. 29
The White House.
Note. Source: (Dibrova, 2024).

Q: How did the North profit from slavery?
A: It is generally understood that slavery was crucial to the economy of the South and, thus,

the United States' economy in general. In the 1830s, for instance, cotton grown by slaves accounted for almost half the value of all exports from the United States (Rodney, 1981). Slavery, however, was also crucial to the North's economy. Some scholars estimate that New York received 40% of U.S. cotton revenue (Thomas, 2019). New England had three times as many textile mills as the entire South. Northern mills manufactured and sold cotton from the South. These mills processed $15 million worth of cotton per year. Northern companies also made money by manufacturing low-grade shoes and clothing for slaves. In Rhode Island, clothes makers' fortunes were tied to the success of slavery since much of their business involved providing cheap, coarse clothing called "Negro cloth" to slavers for their enslaved workers (Beckert & Desan, 2018). Additionally, Northern shipbuilders amassed fortunes building slave ships. According to some writers, 90% of the "Christian" world depended on slave-made goods (Anderson, 1994).

New York City's early history is inseparable from slavery as well. Enslaved Africans in New York helped build New York's City Hall, and Wall Street partially became a major financial center in New York City because it was one of the American colonies' first major slave trading ports (Anderson, 1995). The name "Wall Street" came from the physical wall that enslaved Africans built to protect Dutch settlers from indigenous people's raids. Later, that wall would separate a slave market from nearby residential neighborhoods (Anderson, 1995). By 1711, 40 percent of White New Yorkers' homes had enslaved Black people in them. Some slavers sent the enslaved Black people they owned out to look for additional work. In response to the fears many White people had about numerous Black people traveling through the city seeking extra employment, lawmakers created a centralized slave market where White people could more easily purchase the labor of enslaved Black people (Phillip, 2015).

> *New York City's early history is inseparable from slavery. Enslaved Africans in New York helped build New York's City Hall and Wall Street partially became a major financial center in New York City because it was one of the American colonies' first major slave trading ports.*

Q: Didn't the Northern states hate slavey?
A: At the time of the writing of the Declaration of Independence, slavery was legal in all 13 of the newly formed states (Lockhart, 2019). In total, slavery existed in the North for nearly two centuries.

New Jersey tried to hold on to its residents' legal right to slavery until January 23, 1866, when, in his first official act as governor, Marcus L. Ward of Newark signed a state Constitutional Amendment that brought about an absolute end to slavery in the state (Williams, 2025). So, while White Americans were declaring their freedom from their perceived British oppressors, winning the Revolutionary War, and fighting and resolving the American Civil War, New Jersey still had laws on the books that legalized Black people's bondage. This may not seem as surprising as it initially appears when we consider that if the Mason-Dixon Line, which marked the beginning of the South, had extended east straight across from the top of the Maryland border, it would have run through southern New Jersey.

Q: What was the value of an enslaved Black person in today's dollars?
A: By the 1850s, the price of an enslaved Black female was $1,300, and the cost of an enslaved Black male was $1,800 (Hine et al., 2014). In current U.S. dollars, the price of that enslaved male would be about $72,357.

Q: How profitable was the slave trade in America?
A: The profitability and importance of slavery to America's economy cannot be overstated. Matthew Desmond summarizes the importance of slavery to the U.S. economy:

> Slavery was undeniably a font of phenomenal wealth. By the eve of the Civil War, the Mississippi Valley was home to more millionaires per capita than anywhere else in the United States. Cotton grown and picked by enslaved workers was the nation's most valuable export. The combined value of enslaved people exceeded that of all the railroads and factories in the nation. New Orleans boasted a denser concentration of banking capital than New York City. What made the cotton economy boom in the United States, and not in all the other far-flung parts of the world with climates and soil suitable to the crop, was our nation's unflinching willingness to use violence on nonwhite people and to exert its will on seemingly endless supplies of land and labor (Desmond, 2019).

To bring the value of enslaved people's work to a modern focus, according to U.S. Treasury data, in less than a decade (between 1851 and 1860), enslaved Black people in the South generated an estimated $1.5 billion worth of cotton, which would equate to approximately $54 billion in today's terms (Montero, 2024).

Q: How much money was invested by slavers in the bodies of enslaved Black people?
A: Previously, we examined how much the products enslaved Black people produced were worth, but the value of just the bodies of enslaved Black people was much more than people typically imagine. According to an article from the financial news source Bloomberg:

> The economic value of the 4 million slaves in 1860 was, on average, $1,000 per person, or about $4 billion total. That was more than all the banks, railroads, and factories in the U.S. were worth at the time. In today's dollars, that would come out to as much as $42 trillion, accounting for inflation and compounding interest (Saraiva, 2021).

Q: Since slavery was so profitable, were laws ever changed to help slavers be more successful?
A: Absolutely. There's a long list of laws and political compromises that White Americans created to protect and expand America's slave system, which people might know about (e.g., the 3/5 compromise, the fugitive slave laws, the Missouri Compromise, the Kansas-Nebraska Act, the Dred Scott Decision, the slave codes, etc.). What many people do not know is that the Second Amendment, which modern Americans see as the law that gives citizens the right to bear arms, only exists because of slavery. Southern slavers were terrified that enslaved Black people might rebel and seek revenge. Even Thomas Jefferson admitted he could see himself as the target of a justifiable revolution by his own slaves (NPR, 2021). So, Southern slave states refused to ratify the newly proposed United States Constitution unless it included an Amendment guaranteeing them the right to form armed militias to suppress slave rebellions (NPR, 2021). Carol Anderson explains that the Second Amendment was always meant for the exclusive use of White people:

Even Thomas Jefferson admitted he could see himself as the target of a justifiable. revolution by his own slaves.

> The legal status of African Americans does not have any significant impact on the right to bear arms, the right to self-defense or the right to a well-regulated militia. And the same holds true in this period after the Civil War. You know, we get the Black Codes. A key element in the Black Codes was to disarm African Americans. And this is why you - where you get the rise of these right-wing militias, domestic terrorist groups working with state governments in the South to do that work. You get the slaughter of Black folks, one right after the next (NPR, 2021).

The debates over the Second Amendment today rarely acknowledge the law's origins in the violent oppression of Black people.

Q: Were Europeans the only people to enslave Africans?
A: No. Arabs from the Middle East purchased prisoners of African wars and enslaved Africans from at least 652 to 1890 A.D. (Anderson, 1995).

Q: Why did Arabs want African slaves?
A: Arabs often wanted African women to fill the demand for concubines. Thus, African women in the slave trade outnumbered men 2 to 1 (Anderson, 1995).

Q: How many Africans did Arabs enslave?
A: Scholars estimate that Arabs enslaved 9.64 million African women and 4.75 million African men. Arab slavers killed another estimated 14 to 20 million Africans during the Trans-Saharan slave trade (Anderson, 1995).

Fig. 30
A 19th-century engraving illustrating an Arab slave-trading caravan transporting African slaves across the Sahara.
Note. Source: (Lewis, 2011).

Q: How many Black people died in the Maafa?
A: Too often, people talk only about the 14 million Black people that slavers forcibly exported from Africa on slave ships. Marcus Rediker estimates that of those 14 million people, only 9 to 10 million survived the crossing of the Atlantic Ocean (Jablonka, 2019). However, if we consider the number of Black people slavers killed from start to finish in the journey of captured Africans from Africa to the Americas, the number changes drastically. If we start counting the number of Black people slavers killed from European-instigated conflicts in Africa, to Africans' point of capture, to the Death March, to storage in slave castles, to the journey across the Atlantic Ocean on slave ships, and finally during the seasoning process, that number rises to an estimate of 30,000,000 before enslaved Black people were even fully trained for their first regular day of work on a plantation or farm in the Americas (Stannard, 1992).

Lesson 3: Ending Slavery

> ### Core Concepts
> - Slavery in the U.S. ended due to economic shifts, political pressures, and enslaved people's resistance, including escape, rebellion, and aiding the Union Army.
> - Abraham Lincoln's Emancipation Proclamation was a military decision, not a moral one, and it only freed enslaved people in specific Confederate territories.
> - The notion that White people ended slavery out of kindness overlooks the crucial role Black people played in their own struggle for freedom.

Language in the Lesson

Contraband camps – Unsafe and unsanitary areas near Union bases where many freed Black people lived after emancipation, sometimes in former slave pens.
13th Amendment – The law that abolished slavery in 1865, "except as punishment for a crime," which allowed slavery to continue through imprisonment.
Abolitionist – A person who actively worked to end slavery, especially during the 18th and 19th centuries.
Abraham Lincoln – The U.S. president during the Civil War who opposed slavery but believed Black people were inferior and unworthy of full freedom or equality.
Freedmen's Bureau – A federal organization that helped formerly enslaved Black people transition to freedom by offering food, housing, education, legal help, and medical care.

Q: Did Abraham Lincoln free enslaved Black people and end the institution of slavery in America?

A: Despite popular opinion, to call **Abraham Lincoln** "The Great Emancipator" is an incredible stretch. In *Forced into Glory*, Lerone Bennett, Jr. argues that Lincoln's views on Black people more resemble those of a White supremacist than those of a champion of Black freedom. While it is true that he was against slavery, Lincoln unashamedly believed Black people were inferior to White people. He favored the gradual emancipation of enslaved Black people over 100 years instead of immediate freedom (Bennett, Jr., 2000).

Fig. 31
Abraham Lincoln
Note. Source: (Hicks & Grozelier, 1860).

Q: What did Lincoln think of Black people?

A: While Lincoln was against the institution of slavery, he certainly did not think Black people and White people were equals, as evidenced by this quote from his debate with Stephen Douglass for a U.S. Senate seat:

I will say then that I am not, nor ever have been, in favor of bringing about in any way the social and political equality of the white and black races, [applause]—that I am not nor ever have been in favor of making voters or jurors of negroes, nor of qualifying them to hold office, nor to intermarry with white people; and I will say in addition to this that there is a physical difference between the white and black races which I believe will forever forbid the two races living together on terms of social and political equality. And inasmuch as they cannot so live, while they do remain together there must be the position of superior and inferior, and I as much as any other man am in favor of having the superior position assigned to the white race. (Abraham Lincoln Presidential Library and Museum, 2024).

As President, one of Lincoln's Generals in the War Department, James Samuel Wadsworth, noted that Lincoln frequently spoke of "the nigger question" (Bennett, Jr. 2000, p.14). Another of Lincoln's contemporaries noted that Lincoln spoke of the abolitionists who tried to end slavery in terms of disgust. Ralph Waldo Emerson wrote that Lincoln almost thought emancipation was morally wrong and only used it as a desperate measure to help win the Civil War (Bennett, 2000).

Q: Did Lincoln actually do anything that suggested he was less than sympathetic to Black suffering?
A: In the spring of 1862, Lincoln hesitated to act on the District of Columbia emancipation bill for two nights because he promised an old friend that he would not sign the bill until he could leave D.C. with two of his slaves. Lincoln was also distressed that the law freed enslaved Black people immediately instead of gradually, because immediate freedom meant that White families would suddenly be without cooks and stable boys (Bennett, 2000).

Q: But didn't Lincoln free the slaves with the Emancipation Proclamation?
A: No. Lincoln probably helped to enslave more Black people with the Emancipation Proclamation than he freed. During the Civil War, Congress passed the Second Confiscation Act on July 17, 1862, six months before the signing of the Emancipation Proclamation. The act called for the confiscation of Southern rebels' property, defining rebels as traitors, and freeing all enslaved Black people owned by the rebels (Bennett, 2000). Lincoln's Emancipation Proclamation stopped this act. One day before this act was to take effect, Lincoln signed the preliminary Emancipation Proclamation, which was far less aggressive (Bennett, Jr. 2000). The Emancipation Proclamation postponed the confiscation of rebel property and limited the emancipation of slaves only to specific areas still in "armed rebellion."

Lincoln probably helped to enslave more Black people with the Emancipation Proclamation than he freed.

The Second Confiscation Act would have freed all slaves in Confederate territories. Under Lincoln's Emancipation Proclamation, however, enslaved Black people in states and territories that the Union controlled were not free. Before the Emancipation Proclamation, thousands of Black people in New Orleans, for instance, were essentially freed when the Union army took over the area. If the Second Confiscation Act had been allowed to go into effect, those freed Black people would have remained free, but instead, Lincoln put the Emancipation Proclamation into effect. Since the territory was no longer in armed rebellion, slavers could reclaim those enslaved Black people. Thus, Lerone Bennett, Jr. concludes that "On January 1, 1863, Abraham Lincoln re-enslaved...more Blacks than he ever freed" (Bennett, 2000, p. 13).

Q: If Lincoln did not "free the slaves," who did?

A: Historian Ira Berlin proposed the concept of "self-emancipation," which means that Black people actively claimed their freedom rather than having it bestowed upon them by benevolent White people (Berlin, 2006). Black people's political and military action was the biggest catalyst for America's reluctant destruction of slavery. Black people in America pushed slavery toward its demise in several ways.

Abolitionists

Abolition was the movement to end slavery. Blacks in America began demanding that Congress end slavery as early as 1797. By 1830, Blacks had organized fifty anti-enslavement societies. Black abolitionists worked alone and with White abolitionists to raise funds for the purchase, aid, and legal defense of enslaved Black people, boycott slave-made products, provide security forces for the defense of anti-enslavement rallies, and prevent kidnappings (Karenga, 2002). Black abolitionists established a distinguished speakers bureau to travel and denounce slavery, with Frederick Douglass becoming the most eloquent and influential anti-slavery speaker. Douglass famously said:

Fig. 32
Famed abolitionist Frederick Douglass
Note. Source: (Buttre, 1855).

> Power concedes nothing without a demand. It never did and it never will. Find out just what any people will quietly submit to and you have found out the exact measure of injustice and wrong which will be imposed upon them, and these will continue till they are resisted with either words or blows, or with both. The limits of tyrants are prescribed by the endurance of those whom they oppress (Anderson, 1993, p.76).

Black abolitionists also engaged in a massive anti-slavery publication effort where they disseminated slave narratives (first-hand accounts of the horrors of slavery), anti-slavery newspapers, and persuasive texts like David Walker's Appeal. (Karenga, 2002).

The Underground Railroad

The Underground Railroad was not a physical rail system but rather a method of freeing and transporting enslaved Black people to the North in America or Canada through a network of secret hiding places among homes and churches of anti-slavery advocates. The "Underground Railroad's" most famous "conductor" was Harriet Tubman. Tubman is famous for her repeated daring trips to rescue enslaved Black people. Only armed with a small pistol for protection from slave catchers and to threaten any runaways who were scared to continue the journey, Tubman executed 13 rescue missions, freeing roughly 70 enslaved Black people from Maryland (Larson, 2019)

Though it is not discussed much, enslaved Black people also ran south across the Mexican border to gain freedom. Historian Alice L. Baumgartner estimates that about 3,000 enslaved Black people successfully made it across the border to freedom (Burnett, 2021). Felix Haywood was enslaved in Texas, and in a 1937 interview, he explained why running to Mexico made more sense than running to the North:

Fig. 33
Charlotte Forten Grimké
Note. Source: ("Charlotte Forten Grimké Full." 2013).

There wasn't no reason to run up north," he continued in the interview. "All we had to do was to walk, but walk south, and we'd be free as soon as we crossed the Rio Grande. In Mexico, you could be free. They didn't care what color you was - black, white, yellow or blue. Hundreds of slaves did go to Mexico and got on all right (Burnett, 2021).

Black Women

Though Harriet Tubman is the most famous Black woman abolitionist, she was not alone. Sojourner Truth (1797–1883) was a speaker who fought for the abolition of slavery and effectively connected the issue of slavery to the cause of women's rights. Frances Ellen Watkins Harper (1825–1911) was a free Black woman who was a poet and lecturer whose most famous poem, "Bury Me in a Free Land," became a staple of the abolitionist movement. Maria W. Stewart (1803–1879) was a speaker and writer who challenged slavery, racism, and discrimination against women (Zinn Education Project, 2016). Black women also formed the first female anti-enslavement society, the Salem Female Anti-slavery Society, in 1832 (Karenga, 2002). Charlotte Forten Grimké (1837–1914) was an educator and activist who joined the Salem Female Anti-Slavery Society, fought against slavery, and later taught freed Black people (Zinn Education Project, 2016). These women created models of Black female activism that inspired and paved the way for future women and men who led the struggle for Black freedom (Karenga, 2002).

The Civil War
The pivotal event that led to the end of chattel slavery in America was undoubtedly the American Civil War. Abolitionists effectively elevated the issue of slavery to the forefront of American politics, provoking resentment from Southern states whose economies relied heavily on enslaved Black labor and the goods produced. Several Southern states viewed the Northern abolitionist movement as a threat to their way of life and eventually seceded from the United States to form the Confederate States of America. Predictably, the United States federal government (i.e., the Union) opposed this secession, leading to the outbreak of war.

Q: Don't some people say the South was just trying to protect states' rights, and the Civil War had little to do with slavery?
A: Some people do say this, but it is historically incorrect. Southern leaders explicitly stated that their reason for wanting to create their own nation was to protect slavery. The following is a quote from Alexander Stephens, Vice President of the Confederate States of America, serving under Confederate President Jefferson Davis from 1861 to 1865:

> Our new government is founded upon exactly the opposite ideas [as those of slavery foes]; its foundations are laid, its cornerstone rests, upon the great truth that the negro is not equal to the white man; that slavery, subordination to the superior race, is his natural and normal condition. This, our new government, is the first, in the history of the world, based upon this great physical, philosophical, and moral truth (Dotinga, 2015).

Q: Did any Black people fight in the Civil War?
A: Black people in America fought in every war in which America was involved. Not surprisingly, in the Civil War, most Black soldiers fought on the side of the Union to help end slavery. Once the Civil War started, large numbers of enslaved Black people fled their slavers' plantations and offered their service to Union soldiers. Frequently, the federal government only saw Black people who enlisted in the armed forces as a source of manual labor. Still, by the war's end, Black soldiers served in artillery and infantry but also worked as carpenters, nurses, scouts, spies, steamboat pilots, guards, and surgeons (Weidman, 2016).

Q: How many Black people fought for the Union during the Civil War?

A: Ten percent of the Union Army were Black men (179,000), and 19,000 Black men served in the Navy. Due to the racist beliefs of White commanding officers about the abilities of Black fighters, Black military units were not deployed in combat as often as they could have been. However, Black military units displayed great valor in battles across the South, including most notably, the 54th Regiment of Massachusetts Volunteers, which suffered heavy casualties, losing most of its officers and half of its troops in the assault on Fort Wagner in South Carolina (Weidman, 2016).

Fig. 34
An African American Union soldier with his family.
Note. Source: (United States Library of Congress, 1863).

Q: What difficulties did Black soldiers face while trying to serve in the Union Army?

A: Black people faced a number of obstacles. On the Confederate side, the Confederate army refused to give captured Black soldiers the rights to which all prisoners of war were legally entitled. On the Union side, the army placed Black people in segregated units. The Union Army banned Black soldiers from becoming commissioned officers and paid Black soldiers less money than White soldiers. Thus, America forced Black people to fight a war on two fronts. They had to fight the Confederate army on the battlefield to end slavery and fight the racism of the Union army back in the barracks (Berlin, 1992).

Q: Did any Black people fight on the side of the pro-slavery Confederacy?

A: There are a handful of eyewitness accounts from Union soldiers who said they saw Black people firing arms for the Confederacy, but no Confederate records reference any officers having Black soldiers under their command. Confederate officers and soldiers did, however, force enslaved Black people to follow them to war and provide manual labor. It was not until there were only three months of active fighting left in the war that the Confederate Congress made a law that allowed Black soldiers to fight on their side, but with the clear understanding that they would still be slaves. There is no evidence that the Confederacy formed any Black units as a result of the new law, and Confederate leaders like Robert Toombs, who was the Confederacy's first Secretary of State and a general in Robert E. Lee's army, pushed back on the idea:

> *While there is an absence of clear records of Black Confederate soldiers, there is evidence of small groups of an elite class of free Black people in the South who wanted the Confederacy to win.*

In my opinion, the worst calamity that could befall us would be to gain our independence by the valor of our slaves, instead of our own. If we are conquered by the fortunes of war, we may save our honor and leave the cause to our descendants, who may be wiser and braver than we are and may avail themselves of the accidents of human affairs, and yet win what we are ignominiously throwing away. The day that the army of Virginia allows a negro regiment to enter their lines as soldiers they will be degraded, ruined and disgraced (Smith, 2015).

While there is an absence of clear records of Black Confederate soldiers, there is evidence of small groups of an elite class of free Black people in the South who wanted the Confederacy to win. A free Black landowner in Charleston, South Carolina, said:

In our veins flows the blood of the white race, in some half, in others much more than half white blood, ... Our attachments are with you, our hopes and safety and protection from you. ... Our allegiance is due to South Carolina and in her defense, we will offer up our lives, and all that is dear to us (Litwack, 1979, p. 17).

Q: When did slavery end in the United States?
A: On April 9, 1865, General Robert E. Lee of the Confederate States of America surrendered, effectively concluding the Civil War. While some Confederate commanders held out and did not surrender until shortly thereafter (McPherson, 1988), Lee's defeat signaled the beginning of the end for over 250 years of slavery (Franklin & Moss, 1998). Despite the common belief that slavery ended in June 1865, when enslaved Black people in Galveston, Texas, finally learned of their freedom, leading to the observance of Juneteenth, the federal government formally abolished the institution of chattel slavery with the ratification of the **13th Amendment** in December 1865. Notably, President Lincoln initially opposed the 13th Amendment because it mandated the immediate emancipation of all slaves (Bennett, 1998).

Lesson 4: Reconstruction and Jim Crow

Core Concepts
- After slavery ended, Reconstruction briefly gave Black Americans political power and civil rights, but White backlash destroyed these gains through terrorism, voter suppression, and systemic racism.
- Jim Crow laws enforced racial segregation and second-class citizenship in the South, attempting to control every aspect of Black life.
- Black communities, despite oppression, built schools, businesses, and institutions that laid the groundwork for future civil rights struggles, demonstrating resilience against organized White supremacy.

Language in the Lesson

Convict leasing – A system where Southern states imprisoned Black people for minor offenses and rented them to businesses for harsh, unpaid labor.

Jim Crow – A system of laws and customs that controlled and segregated Black people after Reconstruction.

Ku Klux Klan – A White supremacist group that used violence and terror to suppress Black advancement.

Lynchings – Mob executions of Black people used to enforce racial control and terror.

Reconstruction – The period after the Civil War when formerly enslaved Black people briefly gained rights and protections.

Sharecropping – A farming system where workers use a landowner's land and repay them with a portion of the crops they grow and sell, often under unfair conditions that kept the workers in poverty and debt.

Q: So, life got much better for Black people after the American chattel slavery system ended?
A: While just about everybody in America has some familiarity with the American slave system (or at the very least, they recognize that Americans practiced widespread slavery), fewer people understand the horrors that Black people in America faced shortly after the close of America's peculiar institution. The decisions made by people in power during this period ensured that they embedded White supremacy into the foundation of modern America.

One historian estimates that 25% (one million) of all freed Black people either died or suffered from illness between 1862 and 1870.

Q: What was the condition of freed Black people immediately after slavery?
A: The condition of freed Black people after emancipation was often dire. Most freed Black people possessed no land or money, and Whites continued to exclude them from most economic opportunities in the South, especially while it was still recovering from the Civil War (Foner, 1988). One historian estimates that 25% (one million) of all freed Black people either died or suffered from illness between 1862 and 1870 (Harris, 2012). Numerous freed Black people who survived still faced living conditions similar to slavery:

> Many ended up in encampments called "**contraband camps**" that were often near Union army bases. However, conditions were unsanitary, and food supplies were limited. Shockingly, some contraband camps were actually former slave pens, meaning newly freed people ended up being kept virtual prisoners back in the same cells that had previously held them. In many such camps disease and hunger led to countless deaths. Often the only way to leave the camp was to agree to go back to work on the very same plantations from which the slaves had recently escaped (Harris, 2012).

Q: How difficult was it for Black people to earn a living after slavery?
A: After slavery, Black people with no land of their own often had to resort to entering into labor contracts. This practice was known as **sharecropping**. In a sharecropping arrangement, a landowner allows workers to use their land to grow and harvest crops in exchange for a share of the profit from any crops sold.

The arrangement appears to be beneficial on the surface, as the landowner needs workers and the workers need land. However, the landowners rarely shared profits fairly. They charged workers for tools, seeds, fertilizers, and other farming equipment. However, the interest rates were so high that workers usually ended up owing money at the end of the harvest season. (PBS, 2017). If Black workers quit their sharecropping plantation, lumber camp, or mine while still in debt, they would be arrested and auctioned off to labor camps. White landowners trapped Black workers in jobs that would never let them escape debt and be free. Consequently, fewer than 20% of all sharecroppers ever turned a profit, and that profit could be as little as 9 cents a day (Anderson, 2016).

Fig. 35
A sharecropper collecting cotton.
Note. Source:(Library of Congress, 2024).

Unlike White workers, Black workers were not allowed to seek better wages or work conditions. Additionally, in some places, it was illegal for Black people to be self-sufficient. They were not allowed to hunt, fish, or farm for themselves, which forced Black people to be dependent on Whites for work and food, no matter how unfair and abusive their work conditions were. In some cases, when Black people dared to fight back against abuse at work, White people murdered them, as well as random Black people in the area for good measure (Anderson, 2016).

Q: What was Reconstruction?

A: The end of the Civil War and slavery meant that America would have to rebuild itself as a new nation that embraced freed Black people as part of it when it previously saw them as mere property. Over the next few years, legislators passed a series of laws that transitioned enslaved Black people from property to humans and citizens of the United States. This era became known as **Reconstruction** and was a fleeting moment when it seemed America was veering toward full racial equality.

Q: What did the government do for Black people during Reconstruction?

A: After the 13th Amendment outlawed chattel slavery, the federal government passed several laws that improved Black life. The Civil Rights Act of 1866 overturned the Dred Scott decision and "declared that all persons born in the United States, except untaxed Indians, were citizens of the United States and as such were entitled to equality of treatment before the law..." (Logan, 1965, p.

20). The 14th Amendment to the Constitution was proposed in the same year, further bolstering Black people's claims to citizenship and equal rights. Section 1 of the 14th Amendment states:

> All persons born or naturalized in the United States and subject to the jurisdiction thereof, are citizens of the United States and of the state in wherein they reside. No state shall make or enforce any law which shall abridge the privileges or immunities of the citizens of the United States; nor shall any state deprive any person of life, liberty, or property, without due process of law; nor deny to any person within its jurisdiction the equal protection of the laws.

As part of the Reconstruction Act of 1867, each state that had formerly been part of the Confederacy was required to ratify the 14th Amendment in order to regain admission to the Union (Anderson, 1992).

Q: When did Black people gain the right to vote in America?
A: The Civil Rights Act of 1866 and the 14th Amendment guaranteed some significant rights for Black people, but did not guarantee them the right to vote. The 15th Amendment, however, soon addressed that issue. Ratified in 1870, the 15th Amendment granted male citizens the right to vote regardless of their race or previous condition of servitude. The federal government did not guarantee women's right to vote until 1920 with the passage of the 19th Amendment.

Q: What was the Freedmen's Bureau?
A: In addition to the Reconstruction era's civil rights legislation mentioned above, the federal government established what became known as the "Freedmen's Bureau." The Freedmen's Bureau was responsible for helping Black people adjust from slavery to freedom. John Hope Franklin wrote:

Fig. 36
A Freedmen's Bureau school located in North Carolina.
Note. Source:(Smithsonian National Museum of African American History and Culture, 2021).

> Between 1865 and 1869, for example, the bureau issued 21 million rations, approximately 5 million going to whites and 15 million going to blacks. By 1867 there were forty-six hospitals staffed by physicians, surgeons, and nurses. The medical department spent over $2 million to improve the health of exslaves and treated more

than 450,000 cases of illness. The death rate among former slaves was reduced, and sanitary conditions were improved (1998, p. 229).

The Freedmen's Bureau also helped newly freed Black people find homes, secure labor, and even be transported to less congested areas where they could become self-supporting (Franklin & Moss, 1998). Franklin wrote that the bureau's most notable achievement was providing educational opportunities for Black people. The Freedmen's Bureau played a crucial role in founding a variety of educational institutions, ranging from Sunday schools to industrial schools and colleges. Notably, several prominent Black colleges today, such as Howard University, Hampton University, and Fisk University, received funding from the Freedmen's Bureau. By the time the Freedmen's Bureau finished its educational work, it had been responsible for educating 247,333 students in 4,239 schools (Franklin & Moss, 1998).

Q: What Political gains did Black people make during the Reconstruction era?

A: The Reconstruction era provided a new world of political opportunity. Now that Black men had the right to vote, they became a potent electoral force, particularly in areas where they comprised the majority of the population. The Reconstruction era is responsible for a list of firsts for Black people in politics. P.B.S. Pinchback of Louisiana became the first Black Governor in the United States in 1873, a feat America would not repeat until 1989, when Douglass Wilder won the Virginia gubernatorial race. In 1872, John Roy Lynch became the first Black person to hold the title of Mississippi Speaker of the House. Jonathan Jasper Wright became the first Black person to be elected to the Pennsylvania Bar and the first Black person to serve on South Carolina's Supreme Court (Franklin & Moss, 1998).

Fig. 37
P.B.S. Pinchback
Note. Source:(Brady & Handy, 2006).

Q: How did Southern Whites respond to the progress Black people were making?

A: Even while Black people were beginning to grow accustomed to the taste of freedom, White people in the South actively worked to put limits on that freedom. Shortly after Congress ratified the 13th Amendment, Southern states rolled out the **Black Codes** (Logan, 1965). The Black Codes were the Southern states' attempt to maintain control over Black people, even without the institution of slavery. They resembled the slave codes that governed the movement and legal behavior of slaves before emancipation and included some new tricks. Vagrancy, which the state essentially defined as not working for a White person, was outlawed. Vagrancy laws forced Black people to take jobs with employers who would abuse them, knowing that they could not quit for fear of being imprisoned (Franklin & Moss, 1998).

Q: What were White people's perceptions of Black people now that they were free?

A: Even after Congress ratified the 14th and 15th Amendments, Southern Whites continued to fight to preserve the way of life to which they had grown accustomed. During Reconstruction, Southern Whites painted a portrait of Black people as dangerous animals on the loose. Southern Whites perceived Black people's newfound freedom and growing power as an invasion that they needed to fend off. To this end, White people in the South became determined to establish "home rule," which resulted in Black people becoming the victims of countless acts of terror. The desire to restore White supremacy to full strength in the South led to the rise of a wave of White terrorist groups, including the White Brotherhood, the Pale Faces, the Rifle Clubs of South Carolina, and the most influential group, the **Ku Klux Klan** (Logan, 1965). These groups and like-minded individual citizens unleashed a wave of terror on Black people that would last for nearly one hundred years. Rayford Logan described the worst decades of this period as "The Nadir," meaning the lowest point in race relations (Logan, 1965).

Fig. 38
Ku Klux Klan gathering in Gainesville, Florida in 1922.
Note. Source: ("Klan-In-Gainesville," 2007).

Q: When did Black people start to lose the gains they made during Reconstruction?

A: The Compromise of 1877 was the key event that explains how Black people went from having more power and rights than they had ever previously enjoyed to being reduced to a state that, in some cases, was worse than slavery. In the 1876 Presidential election, the Republican candidate, Rutherford B. Hayes, won the electoral vote but lost the popular vote to the Democratic candidate, Samuel Tilden. There was also a dispute over 20 of the electoral votes. A Republican-led commission investigated the matter and determined that Hayes was the rightful winner. Still, the commission's findings were not final until the House of Representatives, which the Democrats controlled, approved them. To sway Congress toward accepting his legitimacy as President, Hayes gave the Democrats three concessions:

1. Hayes would remove federal troops from the South.
2. The federal government would pay for rail and waterway transportation improvements in the South.
3. Hayes would appoint a conservative Southerner to his cabinet (Danzer, 2002).

With Hayes' removal of federal troops from the South, Reconstruction ended.

Q: What was Jim Crow?

A: After the end of Reconstruction, the South instituted a revamped version of the Black Codes to ensure that Black people would stay in their assigned place, firmly beneath White people. This system was nicknamed "***Jim Crow.***" Jim Crow was a collection of laws and customs that attempted to control every aspect of Black life from the most monumental action to the most minute.

Q: What were examples of the racist laws that White people imposed on Black people in the Jim Crow era?

A: These White supremacist laws that legally oppressed Black people were awesome in their thoroughness. Leon Litwack, in *Trouble in Mind* (1998), gives numerous examples that show the oppressive environment White people in the Jim Crow South forced Black people to live in:

- White lawmakers separated Black people from White people on all means of public transportation. As such, White people forced

Fig. 39
Cover of an early edition of "Jump Jim Crow" sheet music.
Note. Source: (Clay, 2008).

them to sit in segregated waiting rooms and, once on a train, sit in second-class or smoking cars. Some cities also found it necessary to pay for separate streetcars to reduce the chance of a White person having any more contact with a Black person than absolutely necessary.

- Black people were not allowed in the same hotels or restaurants as White people, as their very presence would evoke feelings of disgust in them.
- Black people were not allowed to try on clothes at department stores.
- If Black people were allowed to attend the same movie theaters as White people, they were sometimes required to purchase their tickets from a separate box office, enter through a separate entrance, and sit in the balcony.
- Black motorists were not allowed to pass White motorists on unpaved or dusty roads for fear that White motorists would take it as a sign of impudence or, worse yet, they would splash dirt or mud on them.
- Black and White children were not to share the same textbooks.
- Courts would not allow Black people to be sworn in on the same Bible as White people.
- Black people had separate telephone booths, separate windows for banks, and even separate elevators in some cases.
- Some cities went as far as to separate Black and White prostitutes to prevent them from working in the same areas.
- Black people were not permitted to live in the same neighborhoods as White people.
- Jim Crow even extended into death as Black people were not allowed to be buried in the same cemeteries, and White people sometimes wondered how God could tolerate niggers in heaven (Litwack, 1998).

The examples of Jim Crow laws above serve as only a small example of the detailed list of racial rules White people forced Black people to follow, not only in the South but also in many places in the North. Black people's failure to quickly learn how to navigate this minefield of racism, discrimination, and segregation could easily mean death because of the wrong gesture, word, or look.

Q: How did White people punish Black people for disobeying Jim Crow laws?
A: The most well-known form of punishment was **lynchings**. The word "lynch' means to put to death by mob action without legal sanction or due process of law. As it applied to Black people, lynching was also a means by which White people intimidated Black people into submissive behavior. During

the century after the end of American slavery, lynchings were recurrent throughout both the North and South.

Q: Was there any rhyme or reason behind where lynchings occurred?

A: In *A Rage for Order*, Joel Williamson explained that by the 1890s, lynchings had a definite pattern. Lynchings usually occurred in places where they had happened before, in places where murderers and rapists had been able to escape punishment, and in areas where there was economic uncertainty (Williamson, 1986).

Fig. 40
A 1916 photograph depicting the lynching of Jesse Washington in Waco, Texas.
Note. Source: (Gildersleeve, 2018).

Q: How did the myth of the Black rapist affect Black people during this era?

A: Although there were many laws that Black people could have broken to enrage their White neighbors, almost all lynch mobs used rape as a pretext for violence against Black people (Allen, 2000). Glenda Elizabeth Gilmore wrote that "white leaders deliberately used the threat of interracial sex as a way to unite white men across class lines" (1996, p. 72). The myth of the Black sexual predator united both poor White people and the White elite against a common Black enemy (Gilmore, 1996).

Q: What message were White lynch mobs trying to send?

A: White people showed a consistent tendency to lynch Black people for almost any crime they even thought they might have committed. White people did not intend for Black people to see lynchings as an act against an individual but rather the whole Black race. When Black people refused to follow the demeaning customs of Jim Crow, White people viewed it as a sign that the entire race was becoming too uppity and needed a reminder of where their place was. Thus, when a lynching occurred, it did not matter if a lynch mob found the crime's actual perpetrator. As long as White people punished any Black person, they accomplished their mission (Williamson, 1986).

Q: How did the randomness of lynchings make them even more terrifying?
A: What made lynchings even more terrifying for Black people was the randomness of those chosen for execution (Marable, 1983). Lynch mobs did not always put much effort into finding the actual Black person whom they thought had committed a wrong. Since the purpose of lynching was to send a message to the entire Black community, it did not matter which Black person White vigilantes punished. As long as the Black community got the message to stay in their place, it did not really matter which Black person the White lynch mob killed. Manning Marable, in *How Capitalism Underdeveloped Black America*, wrote that "Terror is not the product of violence alone, but is created only by the random, senseless and even bestial use of coercion against an entire population" (1983, p. 118). Between 1896 and 1946, lynch mobs murdered almost 4,000 Black people, but the effect of those killings spread to everyone in the Black community (Williamson, 1986). Facing each day, not knowing whether their wife, husband, child, or themselves would be the next burnt corpse found hanging in a public space was a daily reality for the entire Black community.

> *Between 1896 and 1946, lynch mobs murdered almost 4,000 Black people, but the effect of those killings spread to everyone in the Black community.*

Q: How horrific were lynchings?
A: Unfortunately, there is no shortage of stories of the horrors of lynchings. Ralph Ginzburg published a collection of newspaper clips on lynchings entitled *100 Years of Lynching in America*, which revealed an astonishing lack of recognition of the humanity of Black people in America. The lynchings that Black people fell victim to varied in their cruelty. In September of 1912, a lynch mob killed a Black man in Princeton, West Virginia, when they mistakenly thought he had attacked a 14-year-old White girl. After the mob executed the man, the town's mayor admitted that he did not come close to fitting the description of the actual rape suspect (Ginzburg, 1988).

In Louisiana, in 1913, a Black man by the name of Watkins Lewis suffered viciously at the hands of another lynch mob:

Stories here tonight tell of a mob of 200 White men, formed in the outskirts of Sylvester last night. Lewis, cringing with fear, was taken from the jail here, placed in a motor car, and whirled to the mob. Not a word was spoken as the little cavalcade formed, and with the Negro in the center marched to a giant tree near the Texas line, Lewis was bound to the trunk.

Fallen trees and branches were heaped about him. Before the fire was lighted, Lewis repeatedly was asked to confess his part in the crime or to divulge the hiding place for a large sum of money said to have been stolen from the postmaster's store. "I didn't do it," he screamed as the flames leaped about him (Ginzburg, 1988, p. 93).

Fig. 41
A 1911 photograph depicting the lynching of Laura Nelson in Okemah, Oklahoma.
Note. Source: (Farnum, 2011).

Q: Were women safe from lynchings at the hands of White people?

A: Women were no safer from White lynch mobs than men were. One of the most horrific incidents of "mob justice" came at the expense of a Black woman in Georgia. Mary Turner was an eight-month pregnant Black woman whose husband was lynched and vowed revenge on those who had killed him. As a result, a mob of several hundred White men gathered and captured Turner. The mob then proceeded to tie her ankles together and hang her upside down. They then doused her clothes with gasoline and set them afire. After her clothes burned from her body, a member of the mob slit her stomach open with a knife and let her premature baby fall to the ground. Someone from the mob then crushed the baby with the heel of his shoe, after which the mob finally killed Turner by firing hundreds of bullets into her body (Litwack, 1998).

Q: Since White people could kill Black women with no consequences, were they also frequently victims of rape?

A: Sadly, the answer is yes. In *At the Dark End of the Street*, Danielle L. McGuire details the history of Black women's pain from and resistance to racial and sexual oppression (2011). The same legal system that allowed White people to kill Black people with impunity allowed them to commit heinous sexual crimes:

On September 3, 1944, Mrs. Recy Taylor, a slender, copper-colored and beautiful twenty-four-year-old mother and sharecropper, walked home from a church revival in Abbeville, Alabama. Just past midnight, a gang of armed white men, kidnapped her off the street, forced her into their green Chevrolet and drove her to a wooded stand a few miles outside town. Herbert Lovett, a 24-year-old private in the United States Army ordered Taylor to undress and get on the ground. "Act just like you do with your husband," he said, "or I'll cut your damn throat." Lovett was the first of six men who raped Taylor that night (McGuire, 2024).

Sadly, Recy Taylor's story is only one of many Black women's stories of unchecked sexual abuse at the hands of White men during this era. In addition to rape, White men frequently sexually assaulted Black women on streetcars, buses, taxi cabs, and other public spaces (McGuire, 2011). Incidentally, one of the best investigators of Black women's rape incidents, including Taylor's, was Rosa Parks of the Montgomery, Alabama, National Association for the Advancement of Colored People (NAACP). Although she has become famous only for having tired feet and refusing to give up her bus seat to a White person, Parks' actual importance lies in her work as the Montgomery NAACP's best investigator. She frequently risked her life traveling through the South to collect information on racial violence. McGuire describes her as "a militant race woman, a sharp detective, and an anti-rape activist" (McGuire, 2024).

Q: Was that type of brutality unusual?
A: Unfortunately, the savagery of White people's attacks on Recy Taylor and Mary Turner was not uncommon. Lynchings were generally public events, not secret rituals. They were often events that entire families attended for entertainment. There are numerous photographs of White people smiling as they posed with corpses of hanged and torched Black bodies. In some cases, White mobs mutilated Black victims by cutting off their fingers, ears, and other pieces of flesh and passing them out to crowds of onlookers as souvenirs (Litwack, 1998).

Fig. 42
Recy Taylor.
Note. Source: (Daily Worker, 2024).

Q: Is it true that people actually sold postcards of lynchings?

A: There are many photographs of White mobs lynching Black people. Even more disgusting is that photographers turned photos of lynchings into postcards for sale. Christina Turner, whose documentary short film *Lynching Postcards: Token of a Great Day* examines the history of these postcards, explains their meaning:

> The postcards were mementos and prideful souvenirs for white people, but they also served as a message, a warning sign, to Black people. They were a proclamation, a way to reinforce white supremacy and keep Black people in their place. So Black people who lived in these communities where lynchings had taken place and where these postcards were created would be well aware of the history (Macabasco, 2022).

In the documentary, historian Terry Anne Scott explains the social significance of lynching postcards:

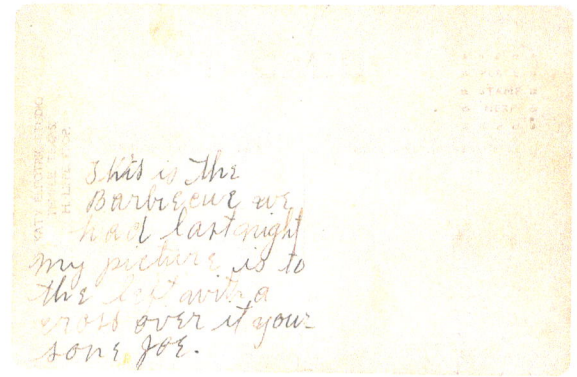

Fig. 43
Postcard depicting the lynching of Will Stanley.
Note. Source: (Crisis, 2009).

> A postcard is an extension of our experience. A postcard allows us to relive that experience. It also allows us to disseminate that experience. People use social media today to show other people what they are doing in their everyday life: "Look what I draw pleasure from. Lynching postcards were used in the same way (Turner, 2021).

Not only were the White mobs that lynched Black people unworried about authorities punishing them, but they were proud to have photographers capture them next to the Black bodies they had just brutally murdered. On top of that, White photographers (who sometimes paid city officials to get exclusive access to photograph the lynching) sold their photos of Black people's deaths for profit (Turner, 2021).

Q: What was "whitecapping?"

A: Historian Carol Anderson explains whitecapping:

Equally vicious was the practice of "whitecapping," which, since the horrors of Bosnia and Srebrenica, we now recognize as ethnic cleansing: In several Georgia and Mississippi counties, where plantations did not dominate the economy, local whites maimed, murdered, and terrorized African Americans and, as the persecuted fled, seized all the land until one could "ride for miles and not see a black face (Anderson, 2016, p, 44).

Q: How difficult was it for Black people to express their outrage over lynchings and other forms of violence against them?

A: White people, of course, expected Black people to remain silent about the unjust murders of their families and neighbors and to accept the rationale that White people were only protecting their communities from dangerous Black creatures. Black people who dared to complain faced fierce resistance from their White neighbors. The famed protector of Black people's civil rights, Ida B. Wells-Barnett, exposed lynchings for what they truly were through her writings. Wells-Barnett argued that White people's fear of Black rapists was an excuse to cover up the real purpose of lynchings, which was to force Black people into an inferior position beneath White people. In 1900, she wrote:

> Our country's national crime is lynching. It is not the creature of an hour, the sudden outburst of uncontrolled fury, or the unspeakable brutality of an insane mob. It represents the cool, calculating deliberation of intelligent people (Hughes, 2022).

As a result of her campaign against lynching, Ida B. Wells-Barnett received numerous death threats that forced her to go into hiding and flee the South temporarily (Gilmore, 1996). At one point, the United States government even tried to intimidate her into silence. After creating and handing out buttons to commemorate twelve Black World War I soldiers whom White mobs lynched while still in uniform, the United States Secret Service visited Wells and threatened to arrest her. The Secret Service told her that she was guilty of treason and that other Black people did not agree with her troublemaking. Wells responded by saying:

> Maybe not. They don't know any better or they are afraid of losing their whole skins. As for myself I don't care. I'd rather go down in history as one lone Negro who dared to tell the government that it had done a dastardly thing than to save my skin by taking back what I have said. I would consider it an honor to spend whatever years are necessary in prison as the one member of the race who protested, rather than to be with all the 11,999,999 Negroes who didn't have to go to prison because they kept their mouths shut (Wells-Barnett, 2020, p. 316).

Q: What challenges did Black people face in addition to violence from their White neighbors?

A: The reward for those Black people who were able to survive during this era was daily humiliation. A collection of scholars combined their efforts to produce a volume entitled *Remembering Jim Crow*, which contains numerous first-person accounts of the trials of living through the Jim Crow era. Ann Pointer recalled having to walk past several closer "White" schools on her way to the school designated for Black children. Pointer had to walk to school because Black people could not use the school buses, even though Black residents' tax dollars helped pay for them. Pointer recalled, "Nothing rode the buses but the whites. And they would ride and throw trash, throw rocks and everything at us on the road and hoop and holler, 'nigger, nigger, nigger,' all up and down the road" (Chafe, 2001, p. 155). Once Black students arrived at school, they encountered additional challenges. Despite their schools being staffed with dedicated professionals who demanded excellence from their students, they were severely underfunded. In one Mississippi school, there were only three teachers for 350 students. At times, the school year for Black children in Mississippi did not begin until November, allowing them to finish picking the year's cotton harvest. In Georgia, the school year for Black children could be as brief as six weeks (Anderson, 2016).

Fig. 44
Ida B. Wells-Barnett.
Note. Source: (Barnett, 2015).

Q: How did White people try to prevent Black communities from voting?

A: The 15th Amendment should have ensured that at least Black men could participate in elections. However, Black voters were soon to find out that laws are meaningless words if no one is willing to enforce them. White people disfranchised Black people in several ways. One such way was literacy tests in which poorly educated Black people would have to read and understand complicated materials that most White people were not able to comprehend (Packard, 2002). White people used the slightest mistake by Black people on the test as an excuse not to allow them to vote.

In addition to literacy tests, the grandfather clause barred Black people whose grandparents had not previously been eligible to vote from voting in current elections. The grandfather clause was particularly troubling for Black people in the South during this period, as most of their grandparents were slaves who, of course, could not vote. In other cases, White people required potential Black voters to pay for the right to vote. By establishing a poll tax, even if it was a small fee, White people knew it would be enough to prevent many Black people from voting. Even if Black people met all the qualifications to vote, White people still had the luxury of forgetting to submit their names as registered voters on Election Day (Packard, 2002).

What is most disturbing is that states considered these tactics legal. Southern states rewrote their constitutions to include laws that would disfranchise Black people. The federal government accepted the argument that electoral processes were a matter for the states to handle. The damage to Black people's political power was drastic. For example, Louisiana experienced a drop from 130,000 registered Black voters prior to the adoption of a new constitution, which imposed various obstacles for Black people seeking to vote, to just 5,000 registered Black voters afterward (Packard, 2002).

Q: Did White people ever resort to violence to prevent Black people from voting and holding offices?
A: There are numerous cases of White people using violence to stop Black people from participating in politics. According to historian Eric Foner, the violent Ku Klux Klan acted as a military force serving the interests of the Democratic Party, wealthy landowners, and people who generally supported White supremacy (Foner, 1990). In 1868, vigilante groups affiliated with Southern White Democrats in Opelousas, Louisiana, murdered almost 200 Black people to discourage the Black community from participating in politics (Boissoneault, 2018). In 1898, a White mob in Wilmington, North Carolina, created a "White Declaration of Independence" and stated that men of African origin would never rule them again. The next day, they murdered 60 Black people and overthrew the legitimately elected government that had both Black and White officeholders (Tensley, 2021). In 1965, 150 White

> *In 1898, a White mob in Wilmington, North Carolina, created a "White Declaration of Independence" and stated that men of African origin would never rule them again. The next day, they murdered 60 Black people...*

Alabama state troopers attacked hundreds of Black people on a March from Selma to Montgomery, Alabama, protesting for voting rights with tear gas, clubs, and bullwhips (National Archives, 2019).

Q: Were children ever victims of violent White supremacists?

A: Sadly, one of the most well-known incidents of White supremacist violence had four little Black girls as its victims. The 16th Street Baptist Church in Birmingham, Alabama, had become a gathering place for Black organizers to strategize ways to revolt against White supremacy. On Sunday, September 15, 1963, at 10:22 a.m., White supremacists exploded a bomb in the church, killing Addie Mae Collins, Carole Robertson, Cynthia Wesley, and Denise McNair while they were attending Sunday School and injuring more than 20 other members of the congregation (16th Street Baptist Church, n.d.). Twelve-year-old Sarah Collins Rudolph was one of the survivors of the attack, but she permanently lost vision in her right eye after the bomb blast blew glass and shrapnel into her face (Robinson, 2023). That same evening, a Birmingham police officer murdered another Black youth, and another child was murdered by a mob of White men (16th Street Baptist Church, n.d.).

Fig. 45
Remains of a stained glass window from the 16th Street Baptist Church after it was bombed.
Note. Source: (Plummer, 2007).

Q: What drove White people to enact all of these horrible laws and practices?

A: Underneath all of the extraordinary controls put on Black life was White people's uncertainty about Black people's humanity. White people saw Black men, in particular, as threats to Southern society. They viewed them as the antithesis of Southern White women. While Southern women were supposed to be beautiful, innocent, and virtuous, many White people saw Black men as hideous, criminal, super-sexual beasts. Some White people went as far as to argue that Black people's natural state was that of an animal. Slavery and Jim Crow laws were necessary to keep, or at least slow down, Black people's regression into their natural state of bestiality (Williamson, 1986).

Fig. 46
D.W. Griffith's star on the Hollywood Walk of Fame.
Note. Source: (Klein, 2010).

Q: How did literature and media help spread the idea that Black people were dangerous during this era?

A: The 1905 novel The Clansman, which D.W. Griffith later adapted into the first blockbuster film, *The Birth of a Nation*, serves as a clear example of media spreading fear of Black people throughout America. *The Birth of a Nation* is a fictitious account of life in the South after the Civil War. The movie presented Black men as sex-crazed animals who split their days between raping White women and destroying the South's political system. The movie concludes with White people erecting a notoriously violent White supremacist organization called the Ku Klux Klan to rescue the South and restore order by putting Black people back into subservient roles. *The Birth of a Nation* was a wildly successful film, and it even received a favorable review from President Woodrow Wilson at the White House. The movie's success revived the Ku Klux Klan, which had nearly faded from existence. The founder of the second Ku Klux Klan, Joseph Simmons, did his best to draw attention to the film:

> On opening night, Simmons and fellow Klansmen dressed in white sheets and Confederate uniforms paraded down Peachtree Street with hooded horses, firing rifle salutes in front of the theater. The effect was powerful and screenings in more cities echoed the display, including movie ushers donning white sheets. Klansmen also handed out KKK literature before and after screenings (Clark, 2018).

Over the next five years, *The Birth of a Nation* was shown across America, inspiring the creation of new Ku Klux Klan chapters nationwide, with membership reportedly in the millions (Clark, 2018).

Q: Who was Ota Benga?

A: Shortly after the publication of The Clansman, an event unfolded in the North that showed just how animal-like White people thought Black people were. In 1904, a group of White men traveled to Africa and captured several Efe men. The Black men were brought back to America and displayed in a cage at the World's Fair in St. Louis. In 1906, after the fair's conclusion, one of the Black men, Ota Benga, was put in a monkey cage for display at the Bronx Zoo in New York. The idea that White people could kidnap Black people and permanently imprison them in a zoo sent shockwaves of terror through the Black community. The ordeal was too much for Ota Benga to handle, as well, as he eventually took his own life at the age of 28 (Evanzz, 1999).

Q: How did Black people try to combat White people's perception of them as less than human?
A: To counteract the notion that they were uncivilized animals, some Black people made special efforts to show White people just how "civilized" they could be. A number of Black people attempted to negotiate a compromise in which White people would grant those Black people who behaved like middle-class White people the privileges of voting and holding political office (Gilmore, 1996). Famed educator Booker T. Washington encouraged Black people to conform to White middle-class standards, remain in the South, and demonstrate that they were as sophisticated, civilized, and hardworking as White people. The problem, though, was that when Black people showed how successful they could be, White people often met them with

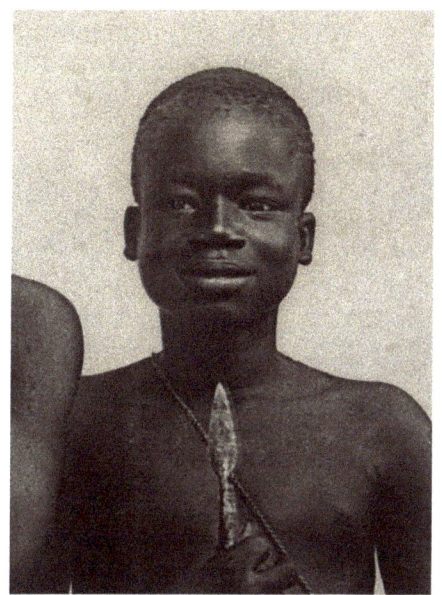

Fig. 47
Ota Benga at the 1904 World's Fair.
Note. Source: (Sisters, 2020).

tremendous violence. In a pattern that Black people would see repeated throughout the country, White people assaulted thriving Black communities. Race riots broke out in Atlanta, New Orleans, Tulsa, and Wilmington, to name a few of the cities where White people attacked Black communities. James Weldon Johnson referred to the summer of 1919 as the "Red Summer" because of all of the blood shed in race riots that season.

Q: But didn't White people like and accept Black people who were "well-behaved" and did everything they expected a good American to do?
A: Black people tried to show that they were as upright, hardworking, and civilized as White people to gain their acceptance, but when they succeeded, White people despised them instead of embracing them. Joel Williamson beautifully summed up Black people's predicament in the following passage about the race riot in Atlanta:

> The great mass of blacks in Atlanta had been doing precisely what whites told them to do working, churching, and quietly managing their own affairs. They had been doing

what Booker T. Washington had advised all blacks to do...more than a decade before. They had cast down their buckets where they were, and now the water came up salty, bitter, and foul (1986, p. 149).

Fig. 48
Booker T. Washington.
Note. Source:
(Schomberg Centre for Research in Black Culture, 2011).

Q: How did the legal system treat Black people during this era?

A: Everything Black people did seemed to be a crime worthy of death or other severe punishment. One of the more severe forms of punishment that White people subjected Black people to was the **convict leasing** system they developed in the South during this period. In *Worse than Slavery*, David Oshinsky examines how, after slavery, various states in the South adopted convict leasing systems that allowed businesspeople to rent workers from prisons. As a result, elected officials passed new laws that allowed Black people to be arrested, convicted, and sentenced to ridiculous terms so that Southern states could profit from their prison labor. For instance, in Alabama, the number of Black people arrested and convicted depended on the coal companies' need for workers. When the coal companies needed more workers, the police would hit the streets and arrest hundreds of Black people for crimes as small as drunkenness or vagrancy, convict them, and sentence them to two to three months of hard labor. Once convicted, they were led to the coal mines to work off their crimes and debts, and by nightfall, they would be working twelve to sixteen-hour shifts (Oshinsky, 1996).

Q: What were the conditions like in the coal mines during the era of convict leasing?

A: In some mines, imprisoned Black people began their three-mile journey to the coal mines at 3 AM and did not finish working until 8 PM, regardless of the weather. Some imprisoned Black people

In some mines, imprisoned Black people worked for weeks or months without seeing the sun. The mines were often filled with standing water around their feet and ankles, which was also the water that imprisoned Black people used as drinking water.

worked for weeks or months in mines without seeing the sun. The mines were often filled with standing water around their feet and ankles, which was also the water that imprisoned Black people used as drinking water. The danger was ever-present as the mines were unclean, disease-ridden, prone to explosions, and contained poisonous gas that got released from the walls as the imprisoned Black miners dug for coal. White jailers and overseers frequently brutally whipped and tortured imprisoned Black people as they had during slavery, and in some cases, even worse (S. Pollard, 2012).

Q: How difficult was it for Black people to buy the land and homes they wanted?
A: Another problem Black people faced as they moved into America's cities was housing discrimination. Again, in a completely legal move at the time, White people created restrictive covenant agreements that prevented Black people from moving into specific neighborhoods. A restrictive covenant is a contract that excludes specific ethnic groups from purchasing a property. When a person buys a property with a restrictive covenant, they agree not to sell the property to people the covenant prohibits. Some covenants went so far as even to limit the number of Black people who could work in a home. The covenants' signers paid a fee, had the agreement notarized to make it binding, and then filed it at city hall, or they had the covenant written into the real estate deed for the property (Stewart, 1996). The effect was the creation of covenant blocks that could legally exclude Black people from residing there.

Q: How is the story of Black people in America different from those of other ethnic groups that experienced discrimination?
A: What makes the story of Black people in America unique is the codification of racism and violence they experienced from White people. That means that the discrimination and abuse Black people experienced from White people was not only legal, but in many cases, it was illegal not to discriminate against Black people. Over many generations, millions of Black people gave their all to America, and in return, the country legalized White people's treatment of them as subhumans. From the Dred Scott decision, in which the court ruled that enslaved Black people were a lesser class of beings that "had no rights which a White man was bound to respect," to Plessy v. Ferguson, in which the Supreme Court ruled that segregation was

The discrimination and abuse Black people experienced from White people was not only legal but, in many cases, it was illegal not to discriminate against Black people.

legal, to the Jim Crow laws, the United States made clear that Black people were unwelcome as equal partners in the American dream.

Q: Did newly arrived European immigrants get treated as poorly as Black people during this era?
A: The codification of racism towards Black people was a particularly hard pill to swallow as they watched White immigrants come to America and receive better treatment than they did. One example of this was the settlement house movement. Settlement houses were places of transition where newly arrived immigrants could live and have workers teach them the skills necessary to function in America successfully. Aid from settlement houses was a courtesy that White people denied many Black people as they moved from the rural South to the urban North, which was equivalent to moving to a new country for many Black people. As more Black people moved to the cities, settlement houses often chose to relocate rather than assist them (Lasch-Quinn, 1993). The settlement housing movement's spurning of Black Americans added insult to injury as Black people who served the country faithfully for centuries watched America pass them over for people who had never previously touched American soil.

Q: How seriously did governments take the classification of people's race?
A: State governments aggressively monitored who could be considered "White." In 1924, Virginia passed the Racial Integrity Act (RIA). The act defined a White person as one who has no trace of any blood other than Caucasian and defined lying about being White on a birth, marriage, or death certificate as a felony (Pearson, 2018). Historian Susan Pearson described how seriously Walter Plecker, the state registrar of vital statistics in Virginia from 1912 to 1946, took his racial gatekeeping:

> Plecker reminded birth attendants that falsifying race on a birth certificate was punishable with jail time. He withheld birth certificates until parents or birth attendants, or the registered people themselves, agreed to "correct" their race, a process that always moved in one direction: from "white" to "colored." If a person refused to agree to reclassification, or if the birth had been registered before the RIA took effect, Plecker issued the certificate with a note appended to the back, explaining that, according to his office, the person was not really white (Pearson, 2018).

Some American anti-miscegenation laws were actually more extreme than the Nazi Nuremberg Laws, particularly in how they defined racial identity (History.com, 2017). For example, while the Nazis defined Jews as people with three or more Jewish grandparents, many U.S. states used the "one-drop rule," classifying someone as Black if they had even a single Black ancestor. Nazi legal scholars found this American approach to be harsher and more obsessive in its racial purity standards than what they were prepared to implement in Germany (Little, 2017).

Q: How valuable was Whiteness during this period?
A: After the passage of the Racial Integrity Act, there were rumors that people sold Whiteness certificates for up to $10,000 apiece. Elizabeth Gillespie McRae notes that even if that was not the exact amount people paid for the certificates, it was still a clear indication of how much people believed Whiteness was worth (McRae, 2018a)

Q: When was the Racial Integrity Act outlawed?
A: By the 1950s, every Southern state made interracial marriage illegal. In Virginia, in 1958, Richard Loving (a White man) married a Black and Native American woman named Mildred. Five weeks after their marriage, the local sheriff arrested the Lovings at 2 a.m. The Lovings pleaded guilty to violating Virginia's interracial marriage ban, and a judge sentenced them to one year in prison. The judge, however, agreed to suspend the sentence if they agreed to leave Virginia and not return for 25 years. The Lovings moved to Washington, D.C., but challenged the Virginia court's ruling. Their case eventually made it before the United States Supreme Court in 1967, which unanimously decided Virginia's ban on interracial marriage was unconstitutional (History.com Editors, 2022).

Q: White men are often associated with racism and violence toward Black people during this era, but where were White women in all of this?
A: Some White women strongly objected to the idea that White men lynched their Black neighbors to protect them. One writer noted the work of White women who rejected

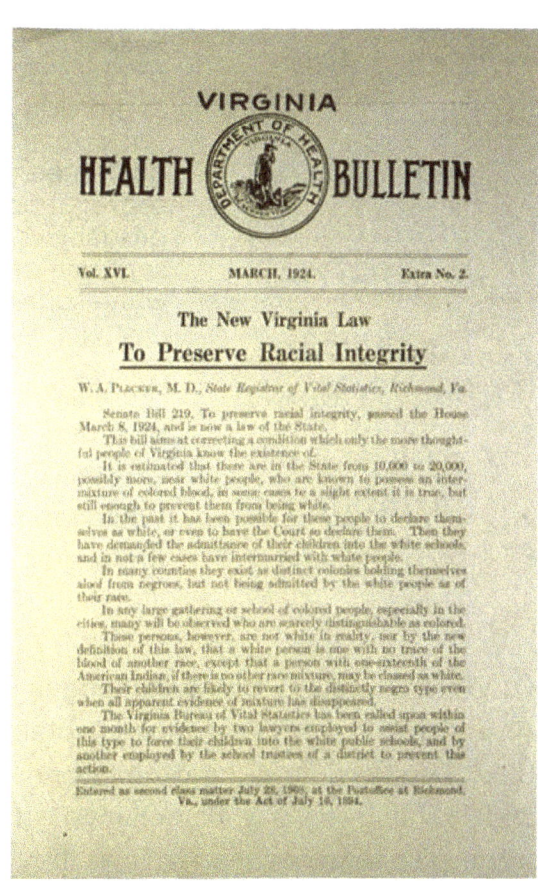

Fig. 49
A copy of the Virginia Racial Integrity Act (1924).
Note. Source: (Virginia Archives, 2015).

the violence happening in their name and wrote, "...the day had come when white women would not allow lynchers to 'hide behind their skirts'" (Dray, 2007, p. 330).

Elizabeth Gillespie McRae points out that other White women, however, were deeply involved in the enforcement of Jim Crow laws. They helped carry racial segregation into every facet of public and private life:

> *White women's acceptance and dissemination of White supremacy provided the foundation that made Jim Crow function even when it violated the U.S. Constitution or federal law.*

Good white mothers reared children who maintained appropriate racial distance, made sure that schools taught a curriculum in line with white supremacist politics, and told stories that educated the larger public on the "naturalness" of racial segregation. Respectable white womanhood relied on the cultivation (at times) of physical, political, and social distance from black men, women, and children. Good white motherhood came to be defined by the same complicated rules except that white mothers had to guarantee that their children learned and adhered to the lessons of segregation. Their duties to the Jim Crow order rested on their progeny. Conversely, if white women and mothers did not follow segregation's dictates, then they threatened the foundation of white supremacy. (McRae, 2018b)

White women's acceptance and dissemination of White supremacy provided the foundation that made Jim Crow function even when it violated the U.S. Constitution or federal law. McRae eloquently wrote that White women's work "shored up white supremacist politics and shaped the segregated state; white women were the mass in massive resistance" (McRae, 2018a, 10:40).

Q: Were there any more challenges Black people faced during this era?
A: The few examples in this chapter represent only a small sampling of the oppression faced by Black people during the century between emancipation and the civil rights movement of the 1950s and 1960s. Every day, Black Americans' White neighbors forced them to live in a world that seemed to despise them no matter what they did. James Weldon Johnson profoundly described this era of Black life in the song that would become known as the Black National Anthem, *Lift Every Voice and Sing*, when he wrote:

> We have come over a way that with tears has been watered
> We have come treading our path through the blood of the slaughtered (Johnson, 1917)

There are no words to accurately describe the pain Black people felt living in an era where it was a crime to be both Black and alive. It was a world where Black people did not enjoy the luxury of having any safe space to exist.

To better understand how long America has legally defined Black people as subhuman and undeserving of full rights, here is a timeline:

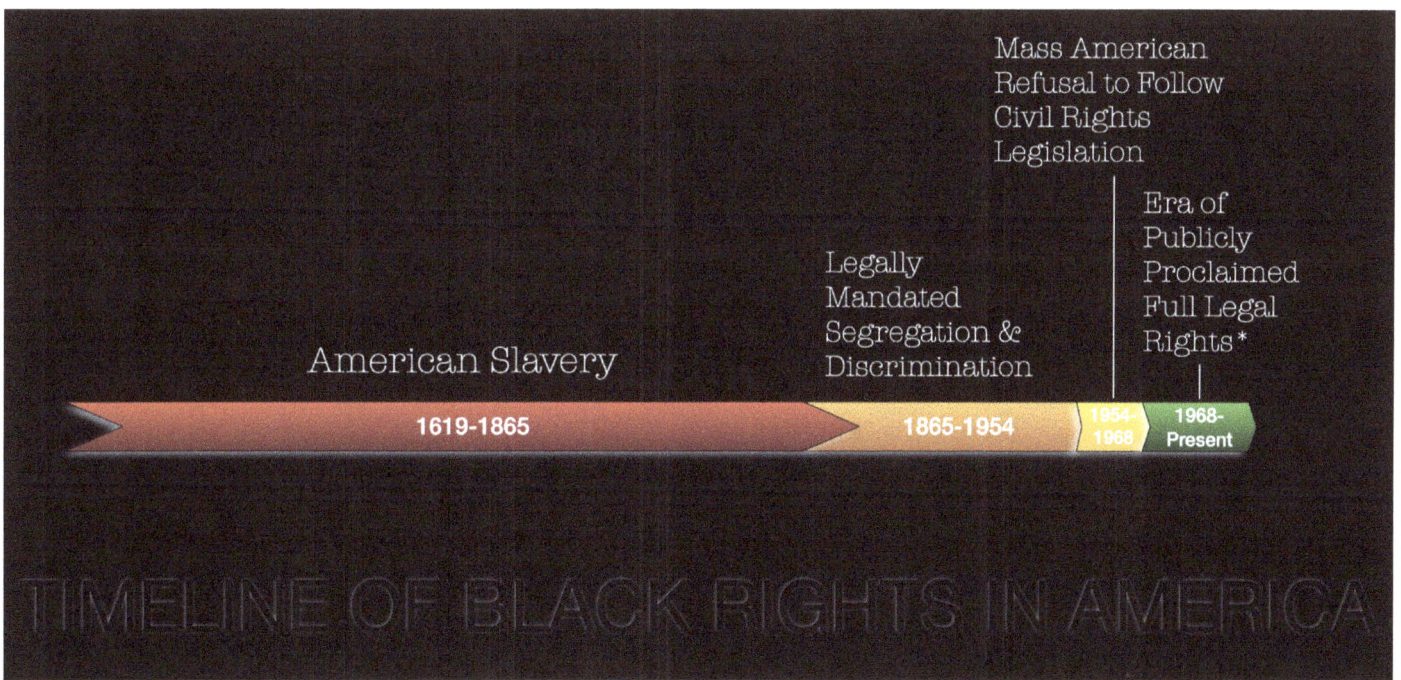

The longest period in American history is the slavery era, which spans from the founding of Jamestown to the end of chattel slavery. America has been a slave-owning nation longer than a free nation. Even after the 13th Amendment ended slavery, the next longest era was marked by legally mandated segregation, discrimination, violence against Black people, and mass White American refusal to follow their own Constitution when it came to Black citizens. The shortest period of Black people's existence in America spans from the passage of the last major Civil Rights legislation to the present day. Out of the 406 years that America has existed as colonies or a nation, White Americans have legally considered Black people as full human beings for less than 60 years.

Lesson 5: Black Resistance and Resiliency

Core Concepts

- Black resistance has always been a force, whether through revolts, escapes, self-defense, or the building of independent schools, churches, and businesses.
- In every era of oppression that White Americans inflicted on them, Black people created new paths forward by refusing to accept the roles and limits White people forced on them.
- Black Americans continue to forge their own path to freedom through strength, intelligence, and self-determination, creating, organizing, and fighting for their rights on their own terms.

Language in the Lesson

COINTELPRO – An FBI program that spied on and undermined Black organizations, labeling them as threats to national security.

FBI – The Federal Bureau of Investigation, whose purpose is supposed to be protecting national security and enforcing federal laws.

The Great Migration – The large-scale movement of Black people from the South to the North and West to escape racism and find opportunity.

Redlining - The discriminatory practice of banks and government agencies denying loans and services to Black neighborhoods, contributing to racial segregation and economic inequality

Revolutionary – A person or idea that challenges unjust systems and fights to create deep, lasting change that empowers the oppressed.

Q: Did Black people accept the abuse their White neighbors continuously inflicted on them?
A: Absolutely not. Black people have and continue to resist every form of abuse and maltreatment from their oppressors. One of the defining features of Black culture is Black people's ability to fight and survive through circumstances that appear seemingly impossible to live through.

Q: So what was the most obvious way in which Black people fought back against the violence during the Jim Crow era?
A: The most significant form of resistance was, at its core, the simplest—just moving away. Two major periods of mass migration saw Black people leaving the South for Northern and Western parts of America, driven by the numerous job opportunities that emerged in cities during World War I and World War II. Between 1910 and 1970, six million Black people made this move (National Archives, 2021). This mass population movement is known as **The Great Migration**.

Q: Since the South was so violently racist, were the White people there happy that Black people decided to leave?
A: Interestingly, White Southerners reacted oppositely, being enraged by their Black neighbors' decision to move. White Southerners' rage turned what should have been a simple escape from White violence into a complex ordeal. White Southerners resented Black people having the audacity to make decisions about their lives without first seeking input and permission from White people. The Great Migration showed that Black people acted with agency, meaning they shaped their own futures rather than just responding to the actions of others:

> Until that moment and from the time of their arrival on these shores, the vast majority of African-Americans had been confined to the South, at the bottom of a feudal social order, at the mercy of slaveholders and their descendants and often-violent vigilantes. The Great Migration was the first big step that the nation's servant class ever took without asking (Wilkerson, 2016).

That idea challenged the whole foundation of the White supremacist South, which was that Black people were docile, simple creatures who happily recognized their need for White people to guide their every action. This mass Black migration showed that Black people were overwhelmingly unhappy with the treatment they received from White people, and they had the intelligence and

The Great Migration led to nearly ten percent of the Black population in the South departing.

ability to plan and organize a massive migration to a seemingly better place (Anderson, 2016).

Q: If White people hated Black people so much, why were they so against Black people leaving the South?
A: Alongside White people feeling offended by Black people moving without their consent, there were significant financial losses associated with Black people leaving the South. The Great Migration led to nearly ten percent of the Black population in the South departing. In just one year, from 1917 to 1918, 500,000 Black people left the South, severely impacting the labor pool. The Georgia Bankers Association reported a loss of $27 million due to the absence of Black labor (Anderson, 2016).

Q: Why were White people so surprised that Black people were unhappy living in the violence of the Jim Crow era?
A: White Americans have a long history of being the last people to realize that they are committing mass acts of racism and violence (e.g., the genocide of Native Americans, chattel slavery, Jim Crow, etc.), and so they were genuinely shocked to discover that Black people were unhappy in the racially oppressive South. They were so shocked that some concluded that "outsiders" must be tricking naive Black people into believing that they were not happy in the South, even when they watched White people lynch their Black neighbors every week. So, White Southerners concluded that corrupt labor agents were to blame for Black people's sudden desire to leave the South (Anderson, 2016). Historian James Grossman wrote:

Fig. 50
Black Floridians moving to New Jersey.
Note. Source: (Delano, 1944).

> They believed, incorrectly, that what was really happening was Black people were being stirred up by labor agents from northern industries coming South to round up Black

workers. This is in part because their genuine belief in the lack of agency of Black people, and that Black people can't possibly be figuring these things out themselves (Clark, 2022).

Q: What were labor agents?
A: Labor agents were individuals hired by companies to assist Black workers in finding employment in the North and West. They were essentially recruiters who informed Black people about job opportunities and assisted them in relocating from the South.

Q: How did White Southerners try to slow the Black migration out of the South?
A: White Southerners went to incredible lengths to stop Black people from abandoning the South. State and municipal governments passed a series of laws that made it difficult for labor agents to operate. In Macon, Georgia, labor agents were required to obtain a $25,000 labor recruiting license to operate legally in the city. That would be roughly $560,000 in 2024. Labor agents were also required to get recommendations from ten ministers, ten manufacturers, and twenty-five other businesspeople. The Georgia state legislature declared labor agent recruiting a felony, and violators could face sentences of three to seven years in prison. If labor agents were caught operating without a license in Jacksonville, Florida, the government could fine them $600 (approximately $14,000 in 2024) and impose a sixty-day jail sentence. In Montgomery, Alabama, the authorities would fine any person encouraging Black workers to leave $100, and they could also be sentenced to six months of hard labor (Anderson, 2016).

Aside from ridiculous laws, Black labor agents' very lives were at risk simply for trying to help Black people get better jobs. Carol Anderson in *White Rage: The Unspoken Truth of Our Racial Divide*, quotes a Black labor agent who said:

> That door swung open and there was two great big, three great big red-faced guys ... Now they had a bullwhip on they shoulder and a rope and a gun in each of their hands. And those pistols, them barrels looked like shotguns, you know? They gonna kill every so-and-so Negro that they found had a pass. Well, so they searched us one by one and they searched me ... Had they pulled off my shoe, that'd been it for me. Because they swo' they was gonna kill the one who had it. Yeah, it was in the toe of my shoe (Anderson, 2016, p. 48).

Q: So, White people were even willing to break the law to use violence just to stop Black people from leaving to find better jobs?

A: Sadly, yes. On numerous occasions, White people sabotaged trains they suspected were carrying Black workers out of the South. White people wrecked train schedules by stopping trains from moving if they had Black passengers moving out of the South on them. This happened even when the country depended on efficient train movement to move supplies during World War I. White people were willing to delay the delivery of supplies to soldiers during the war just to prevent Black people from getting better jobs and homes. In Mississippi, the federal government had to step in and arrest someone for holding up the trains (Anderson, 2016).

Q: Did the police try to protect the rights of Black travelers?

A: Law enforcement was of little help to Black travelers. Sometimes, the police would arrest Black travelers at train stations and hold them until the trains left. In Albany, Georgia, the police ripped up Black people's legally purchased train tickets. Police in Jacksonville arrested Black people trying to leave to get better jobs. In Memphis, Tennessee, the police arrested 26 Black men for attempting to leave and sentenced them to work on a plantation in Arkansas. In other locations, ticket agents simply refused to sell tickets to Black travelers (Anderson, 2016).

Fig. 51
The Arthur family arrives in Chicago two months after two of their family members were lynched in Texas.
Note. Source: (Chicago Defender, 1920).

Q: Besides labor agents, in what other ways did Black people discover the opportunities in the North?

A: Black newspapers played a crucial role in disseminating information about the benefits of relocating North to the Black community. The *Chicago Defender*, Chicago's primary Black newspaper, advocated for Black migration. The *Chicago Defender* informed Black people that they did not need to prove their worthiness to the South; instead, the South needed to demonstrate its value to them. Due to its impact, some Southern cities prohibited the *Chicago Defender* and threatened to imprison anyone found with a copy. Laws against the *Chicago Defender* only heightened its underground popularity within the Black community, spreading through churches, mail, and barbershops. Pullman Porters, Black men who worked as waiters on upscale trains, distributed the *Chicago Defender* nationwide during their travels, leaving copies in the cities they visited (Anderson, 2016).

Fig. 52
A paperboy carrying copies of the *Chicago Defender*.
Note. Source: (Delano, 1942).

Q: Doesn't this go against the idea of the American Dream and American capitalism?
A: Yes. Capitalism is supposed to allow workers to sell their labor to the highest bidder and is an essential part of the so-called American dream. White people inflicted intense systemic racism and violence on Black people who simply sought to leave their lower-paying jobs and move to a place with better living and working conditions. White people can take for granted the ability to accept any job that is available to them. In contrast, Black people have not always had that privilege in America.

Q: Were Black people intimidated and chose not to leave?
A: Quite the opposite. White people's violent resistance made Black people want to leave the South even more, and the number of Black Southerners leaving increased. Anxious Black Southerners would not even let White people know that they were leaving. Some left without getting their last paychecks, while others would leave tools in the fields and flee. Some Black people even hitched rides on freight trains. Black people knew the North was not perfect, but it was better than what they were experiencing in the South (Anderson, 2016).

Q: Which cities experienced an increase in Black populations due to the Great Migration?
A: From 1910 to 1920 alone, the Black population of New York increased 66%, Chicago's Black population increased 148%, while Philadelphia and Detroit's Black populations increased a whopping 500% and 611%, respectively (Zapata, 2010).

Isabel Wilkerson sums up the demographic effect of the Great Migration:

The refugees could not know what was in store for them and for their descendants at their destinations or what effect their exodus would have on the country. But by their actions, they would reshape the social and political geography of every city they fled to. When the migration began, 90 percent of all African-Americans were living in the South. By the time it was over, in the 1970s, 47 percent of all African-Americans were living in the North and West. A rural people had become urban, and a Southern people had spread themselves all over the nation (Wilkerson, 2016).

Q: Were Northern and Western cities the paradises that Black migrants from the South hoped they would be?

A: Sadly, they were not. Racism, discrimination, and violence were waiting for Black migrants in their new lands, just in a different form from the way they presented themselves in the South. Black people in the North, however, did regain access to the right to vote, and some also gained increased access to education. But the cities they now called home were no more loving than the rural communities they left behind. Even as far north and west as Oregon, Black people experienced "sundown towns" where White people banned Black people from being in their towns after dark. The constitution of Oregon banned Black people from even entering the state until 1926 (Wilkerson, 2016).

Wherever Black people settled, they found that only the lowest-paying and most dangerous jobs were available to them. Many White workers' unions banned Black workers, so companies used Black workers as strikebreakers who took the jobs of White workers on strike. This made White unions despise Black workers even more (Wilkerson, 2016).

Q: How did White people's denial of Black people's access to homes in better neighborhoods during this period affect America today?

A: Government policies and White segregationists created many of many poor and under-resourced neighborhoods where Black people live today, as well as the suburbs

Fig. 53
A protester stands in front of a milk company in Chicago.
Note. Source: (Vachon, 1941).

predominantly occupied by White people. The Federal Housing Administration (FHA), established in 1934, refused to insure mortgages in and around Black neighborhoods. However, it provided subsidies to developers who mass-produced new suburban neighborhoods with the condition that only White people could reside there. To maintain property values in these White suburbs, the FHA recommended building walls and highways to separate White neighborhoods from those of Black people (Gross, 2017).

During this period, Americans could buy homes at affordable prices, which later appreciated significantly in value. The Home Owners Loan Corporation (HOLC) and the Federal Housing Administration guaranteed mortgages to encourage banks to lend money to Americans after the Great Depression. Because these government agencies agreed to cover loans for those who defaulted on their mortgage payments, banks became more willing to lend to people who would normally be denied mortgage approvals. However, for many Black people, the HOLC and FHA implemented "**redlining**" policies that continue to ravage the Black community today. These government agencies color-coded neighborhoods on maps, assigning shades of green to the most desirable areas, which were predominantly White commercial zones, followed by wealthier White residential neighborhoods. They marked the most undesirable neighborhoods in red, which were predominantly Black. They then denied insured mortgages to residents in Black neighborhoods as "Negroes" were automatically classified as high risk (NPR, 2018). Consequently, Black people were unable to access loans and insurance necessary to purchase and improve property in their own neighborhoods. Additionally, these same government agencies refused to insure mortgages for Black applicants seeking to buy homes in White neighborhoods. As a result, the federal government and banks effectively barred Black people from purchasing homes in the prime areas where

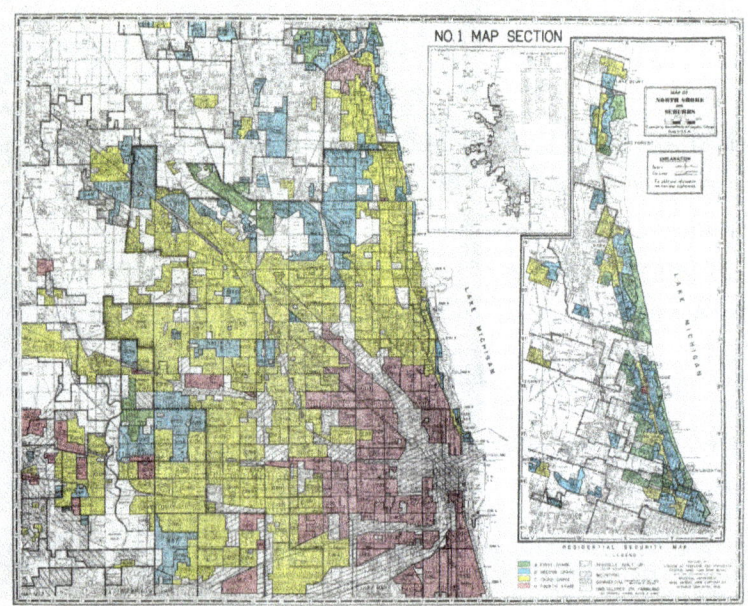

Fig. 54
Chicago redlining map.
Note. Source: (Zelasko, 2012).

White people were approved for insured mortgages (Gross, 2017).

Q: What was the impact of these racist housing policies?
A: The impact of racist housing policies was profound. Black people either had to rent their homes or take on unconventional mortgages with horrible interest rates (NPR, 2018). Consequently, Black Americans' wealth today is only approximately 5% of that of White Americans. Richard Rothstein explains the enduring effects of this discrimination:

> African-American families that were prohibited from buying homes in the suburbs in the 1940s and '50s and even into the '60s, by the Federal Housing Administration, gained none of the equity appreciation that whites gained. So ... the Daly City development south of San Francisco or Levittown or any of the others in between across the country, those homes in the late 1940s and 1950s sold for about twice the national median income. They were affordable to working-class families with an FHA or VA mortgage. African-Americans were equally able to afford those homes as whites but were prohibited from buying them. Today those homes sell for $300,000 [or] $400,000 at the minimum, six, eight times the national median income…(Gross, 2017).

In other cases, restrictive covenants kept Black people out of neighborhoods. In Chicago, for instance, restrictive covenants kept Black people out of 85% of the city. These conditions forced many Black people to live in overcrowded neighborhoods that were the opposite of the paradise Black Southerners dreamed of when they took flight. When Black people ignored racist laws and traditions and dared to live outside the zones White people prescribed for them, White people met them with violence (Wilkerson, 2016).

Q: Was moving out of the South worth it for Black people?
A: Despite clear challenges, Black people made significant progress by moving out of the South. They gained increased access to education, which contributed to securing better jobs. In 1940, the average wage of a Black man was only 40% of what White men earned. By 1970, that figure had risen to 70%, which, although still not equal to those of White men, was nearly double what Black men had previously earned. Moreover, when comparing earnings, Black men in the North were making three times as much as their counterparts in the South in 1940. It is worth noting that evidence suggests that the arrival of Black workers from the South, who were willing to work for lower wages, led to a potential wage reduction for Black workers already in the North (Boustan, 2018).

Q: So, how did Black people's gains in physical and financial freedom help them resist oppression?
A: Black people's gains in disposable income and voting rights, combined with their spread across the country, led to the creation of numerous organizations that advocated for their rights and protection.

Q: I often hear about Martin Luther King, Jr., and nonviolence, but were there any individuals or organizations that took a different approach to combating White racism?
A: Many organizations strongly advocated for Black people to defend themselves in every way possible, including the use of violence. American schools generally do not discuss these organizations in a serious manner; therefore, we must introduce some of them here.

Q: What was the Colfax Massacre?
A: The Colfax Massacre occurred in the context of the fiercely contested Louisiana gubernatorial election of 1872, which resulted in rival governments claiming legitimacy. Radical Republicans, who sought to uphold Reconstruction policies and Black political participation, clashed with White Democrats intent on restoring White supremacy through "home rule" (Keith, 2011).

Fig. 55
Illustration of the Colfax Massacre from Harper's Weekly.
Note. Source: (Harper's Weekly, 1873).

On April 13, 1873, the defining moment in Black resistance against White supremacist violence during Reconstruction took place. Confronted with the threat of White paramilitary groups seeking to dismantle local Republican governance, an armed Black militia, consisting of about 150 men, took strategic defensive measures by fortifying the courthouse in Colfax, Louisiana. These defenders refused to passively accept violent threats from White supremacists. They possessed government-issued Enfield breech-loading rifles and ammunition provided by the Reconstruction-era Republican government, which they aimed to use to protect their civil rights and political power (Keith, 2008).

Recognizing the strength of this organized Black resistance, White supremacists mobilized an even larger force of around 165 armed men, bringing with them a stolen steamboat cannon, which they loaded with metal scraps and slugs to bombard the fortified Black positions. The early phase of the battle was a genuine military engagement, with shooting and casualties on both sides as Black fighters attempted to hold their position (Keith, 2008).

The turning point came when the White attackers outflanked the Black defenders, forcing them to retreat into the courthouse. Even then, the Black militia continued to resist, refusing to surrender despite being outnumbered and outgunned. Eventually, the White mob defeated the Black militia. Then, in a violent frenzy, the White mob set the courthouse on fire, and as the Black fighters tried to extinguish the flames or escape, the mob systematically shot and killed them. The violence escalated further after a White supremacist leader, dressed in Klan-like regalia, was shot, enraging the White attackers. In retaliation, the White mob brutally murdered the Black fighters they captured and lynched Black men near a pecan tree, later glorifying these killings in White supremacist lore. Within a short span of time, the White mob had claimed the lives of an estimated 150 Black people (Keith, 2008).

Despite being outnumbered and eventually overrun, the Black militia's determined resistance challenged the violent attempt to strip them of their rights. Their willingness to take up arms and defend their political freedom was an extraordinary act of defiance in the face of extreme racial terror (Keith, 2008).

Q: Was anyone in the White mob punished?
A: Ultimately, none of the men in the White mob were punished. After initially being convicted, the United States Supreme Court overturned lower federal courts' rulings. In *United States v. Cruikshank*, the Supreme Court ruled that only states, not the federal government, could punish those responsible in local incidents. Since many Southern states refused to punish White supremacists for their violent actions, they grew bolder, and Black people faced more violence and discrimination. This decision weakened Black rights gained during Reconstruction and led to the rise of Jim Crow laws, which enforced segregation and blocked Black voting rights. Without federal protection, racial violence continued unchecked. For years, the massacre was misrepresented, with some even

celebrating the White attackers. Only recently have efforts been made to correct the history and honor the Black victims. (Keith, 2011).

Q: Who were the Deacons for Defense?
A: The deacons for Defense was a Black self-defense organization that formed in Louisiana after the Black community recognized that local police would not protect them from attackers or deter racial violence from White people. The Deacons armed themselves and dedicated themselves to safeguarding their community and the civil rights workers who visited their area. Charles Sims, the founder of the Deacons for Defense, asserts that the organization's local successes led to the establishment of 53 chapters across the country during its height of influence. The Deacons served as bodyguards for the Student Nonviolent Coordinating Committee (SNCC) and the Southern Christian Leadership Conference (SCLC) in Mississippi during James Meredith's 1966 march against fear. They also protected Martin Luther King Jr. while he traveled to preach at a funeral in the Delta region of Louisiana. Sims effectively captured the Deacons' attitude regarding some other Black organizations that spoke of Black Power by saying, "I don't see nothin' they was doin' to even be talking about Black Power. The Black Power, we had it. In them thirty rounds of ammunition on a man's shoulder, we had the Black Power" (Raines, 1977, pp. 422-423).

Fig. 56
A button advocating for the release of Huey Newton.
Note. Source: (Schomburg Center for Research in Black Culture,1967).

Q: Who were the Black Panthers?
A: Huey P. Newton and Bobby Seale established the **Black Panther Party for Self-Defense** in 1966 in Oakland, California. The Black Panthers formed armed patrols that monitored the police in Oakland by following officers as they patrolled Black communities to ensure that they were not violating any laws (Karenga 2002). The Black Panthers' underlying philosophy initially centered on Black nationalism, but it would evolve into **Revolutionary** socialism and ultimately into intercommunalism (Anderson, 2011). The Black Panthers' original ten-point program laid out their goals:

1. We want freedom. We want power to determine the destiny of our black community.
2. We want full employment for our people.

3. We want an end to the robbery by the white man of our black community.
4. We want decent housing, fit for shelter of human beings.
5. We want education for our people that exposes the true nature of this decadent American society. We want education that teaches us our true history and our role in the present day society.
6. We want all black men to be exempt from military service.
7. We want an immediate end to police brutality and murder of black people.
8. We want freedom for all black men held in federal, state, county, and city prisons and jails.
9. We want all black people when brought to trial to be tried in court by a jury of their peer group or people from their black communities, as defined by the Constitution of the United States.
10. We Want Land, Bread, Housing, Education, Clothing, Justice, and Peace (Black Panthers, 1966).

Although the Black Panthers began with armed patrols of local police, they quickly expanded the scope of their work and established chapters across the country that aimed to address as many challenges facing the Black community as possible. To this end, they created and maintained numerous programs for the Black community. Here are just a few of the programs they list as having operated:

- Free Breakfast for Children Program
- Free Ambulance Program
- Bussing to Prisons Program
- Free Clothing Program
- Free Commissary for Prisoners Program
- Free Dental Program
- Free Employment Program
- Free Food Program
- Free Optometry Program
- Free Pest Control Program
- Free Shoe Program
- GED Classes
- Drug/Alcohol Abuse Awareness Program
- Free Furniture Program
- Free Health Clinics
- Free Housing Cooperative Program
- Legal Clinic/Workshops
- Liberation Schools
- Martial Arts Program (Black Panther Party Alumni Legacy Network, 2025).

Q: What role did women play in the Black Panther Party?

A: Women played a crucial yet often overlooked role in the Black Panther Party, reshaping the movement from within and leading many of its most significant initiatives. By the early 1970s, women constituted approximately two-thirds of the Black Panther Party's membership, a fact that is frequently overshadowed by the prevailing public image of militant Black masculinity. Historian Ashley Farmer points out that female members, such as artist Tarika Lewis, challenged conventional gender roles by depicting women as empowered, armed revolutionaries and reimagining leadership within Black liberation movements. Their contributions extended beyond visuals as women also helped create programs addressing community needs, such as free food and healthcare, illustrating a broader revolutionary agenda that intertwined gender, race, and class struggle (Clayman Institute, 2014).

Fig. 57
A flyer promoting the Free Food Program of the Black Panther Party.
Note. Source: (Collection of the Smithsonian National Museum of African American History and Culture, 1972).

Rank-and-file women formed the backbone of the Black Panther Party's daily operations, organizing protests, managing survival programs, and handling communications. They often endured grueling hours under dangerous conditions, driven by a fierce commitment to protecting and uplifting the Black community. Figures like Delores Henderson and Joyce Lee, among others, executed essential party work, from preparing meals for children to attending rallies and conducting security patrols. Despite experiencing internal sexism, these women persisted and demanded respect for their contributions, embodying the Panthers' revolutionary principles (Dixon, 2019).

The women-led community programs, such as the Free Breakfast for Children Program, the People's Free Medical Clinics, and sickle-cell anemia testing, embodied the Black Panther Party's commitment to grassroots service and self-determination. Ericka Huggins, the Party's longest-serving female member, emphasized that this work was not merely a political performance but an act of "service to humanity." These programs, which depended on women Panthers, provided direct aid while challenging systemic neglect by state institutions (O'Hagan, 2022).

As the state targeted male leaders through arrests and violence, women increasingly took on leadership and organizational responsibilities (Dixon, 2019). Black women played a crucial role in the Black Panther Party, not only by supporting its daily activities but also by shaping its political direction and legacy. Leaders like Kathleen Cleaver, who served as communications secretary, and Elaine Brown, who led the Party from 1974 to 1977, demonstrated the importance of women's leadership despite sometimes facing sexism within the organization. Fredrika Newton worked to maintain the Black Panther Party's legacy through the Huey P. Newton Foundation, while Charlotte Hill O'Neal helped expand the movement's reach by establishing a headquarters in Tanzania. Even cultural icon singer Chaka Khan became a member at the age of 16 after running away from home and befriending legendary Chicago Black Panther leader Fred Hampton (White, 2016).

The experiences of women in the Black Panther Party highlight how revolutionary activism empowered them both individually and collectively. For many, including Carol Henry and Barbara Easley-Cox, the Black Panther Party offered a space for profound political awakening and solidarity. Former Black Panther Angela Davis has noted that women's contributions were frequently overlooked because of the media's emphasis on sensational images of male militancy; however, it was women who truly ensured the Black Panther Party's survival and relevance (O'Hagan, 2022; Clayman Institute, 2014; Dixon, 2019).

Q: Did the Black Panthers ever get into armed conflict with the police?
A: Despite the overwhelming good the Black Panthers were providing for Black communities, law enforcement saw them as a threat that they needed to neutralize. J. Edgar Hoover, who directed the Federal Bureau of Investigation (**FBI**), labeled the

Fig. 58
FBI photograph of Elaine Brown.
FBI photo of Elaine Brown.
Note. Source: (FBI, 1970).

Black Panthers as the number one threat to America's internal security and worked tirelessly to criminalize them (Saunders, 2023).

Before sunrise on December 8, 1969, over 300 Los Angeles police officers launched an attack on the Panther headquarters and burst through the front door. The Black Panthers inside were aware of the impending attack and were ready to defend themselves. The Panthers fortified their headquarters with sand-filled walls and sandbagged bunkers to block incoming bullets from the police. Bernard Arafat, who was a 16-year-old member of the Black Panthers, shared his memory of the event with the San Francisco Bay View newspaper:

> I had been relieved from doing security on the roof by Gil and was awakened in the library just before all hell broke loose. Police explosives demolished walls and furniture, ripping portions of the ceiling off. The building was saturated with tear gas and thick smoke. Broken glass and fragments flew through the air, shattered plumbing pipes. Panthers moved about returning fire, and hurled explosives from the windows. Automatic weapons fire repelled the assault for hours (Saunders, 2023).

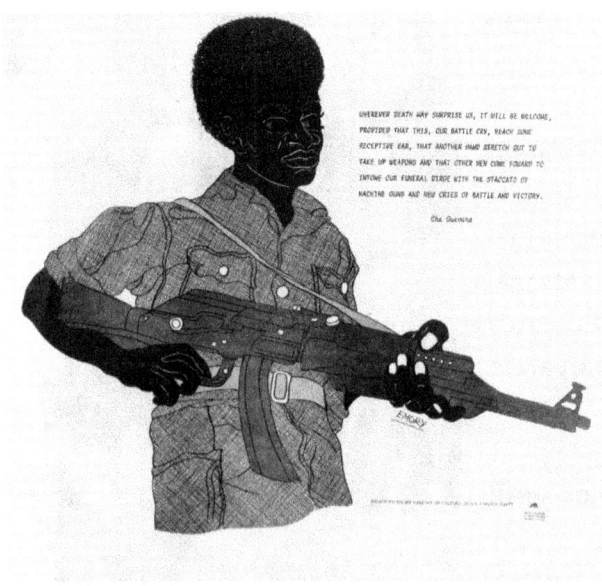

Fig. 59
Revolutionary artwork by Emory Douglas, the Black Panther Minister of Culture.
Note. Source: (Douglas, 1965).

When the police realized that the Black Panthers would not submit quietly, they brought a tank to crash through the Panthers' headquarters. By this time, morning had arrived, and thousands of Black people gathered at the site of the attack, cheering and supporting the Black Panthers (Saunders, 2023). Ultimately, the thirteen Black Panthers who defended against the initial 350 police officers, which included the first-ever SWAT team, surrendered without any casualties, although six were injured. They managed to injure four SWAT team members during the confrontation as well (Fleischer, 2019).

The state charged the Black Panthers with 72 crimes, including assault with a deadly weapon and conspiracy to murder policemen. The Black Panthers' lawyers, which included Johnnie Cochran, argued that the

Panthers had acted in self-defense as the police had entered the Panthers' headquarters violently and without a warrant. The jury agreed and found the charged Black Panthers not guilty on almost every charge. Unfortunately for the Black Panthers, though, they would continue to be violently attacked by law enforcement agencies throughout their entire existence, which ended in 1982 (Fleischer, 2019).

Q: What was the Black Liberation Army?
A: The Black Liberation Army (BLA) was a revolutionary organization that splintered from the Black Panthers and maintained the following principles:

> That we are anti-capitalist, anti-imperialist, anti-racist and anti-sexist.
>
> That we must of necessity strive for the abolishment of these systems and for the institution of Socialistic relationships in which Black people have total and absolute control over their own destiny as a people.
>
> That in order to abolish our system of oppression we must utilize the science of class struggle, develop this science as it relates to our unique national condition (Coordinating Committee: The Black Liberation Army, 1976).

Q: What revolutionary actions did the Black Liberation Army undertake?
A: The Black Liberation Army (BLA) included members of the Black Panthers who believed in the necessity of armed revolution. They criticized the Black Panther Party for shifting its focus towards community survival initiatives and mainstream political activities. As an independent organization, the BLA made its presence known through confrontations with police in cities such as Atlanta, St. Louis, and San Francisco; however, it is primarily recognized for its clashes with law enforcement in the northeastern United States (Rosenau, 2013).

Fig. 60
Black Liberation Army logo.
Note. Source: (Black Liberation Army, 1970).

The BLA viewed the police as an occupying force in Black communities. In 1971, they launched a series of attacks against the New York Police Department (NYPD) in retaliation for what they perceived as repeated incidents of police brutality. In May of that year, BLA gunmen ambushed two police officers who were guarding Manhattan District Attorney Frank Hogan's apartment, as he had previously prosecuted members of the Black Panthers in a high-profile case. On May 21, 1971, two NYPD officers were shot and killed in Harlem, followed by the murder of a Philadelphia Park Police officer in August 1971. Additionally, BLA members robbed a bank in Queens, New York, and threw a grenade at a pursuing NYPD squad car. The BLA claimed responsibility for the murders of two NYPD officers in 1972 and was linked to several shootings of police officers in 1973 (Rosenau, 2013).

Q: What is the most notable event associated with the Black Liberation Army (BLA)?
A: Most famously, in 1973, Assata Shakur (formerly known as Joanne Chesimard) and two other BLA members were involved in a gunfight on the New Jersey Turnpike that left a state trooper dead. The State of New Jersey convicted Shakur of murder and sentenced her to serve a life sentence plus 33 years. Shakur and her lawyers contend that they were never given a fair trial. One writer explains:

> There is much evidence to suggest the trial was not fair: transcripts of the jury selection show at least two of the jurors expressed prejudice before the start of the trial. There was evidence that the offices of the defence team were being bugged, and materials relating to her case that went missing from the home of her late lawyer Stanley Cohen were later found with the New York City police (Adewunmi, 2014).

Convinced that the all-White jury that convicted her either did not hear or ignored the substantial evidence that would have cast doubt on her conviction, she escaped. Three armed BLA members posing as visitors were able to rescue her from the Clinton Correctional Facility for Women in Union Township, New Jersey. After Shakur escaped prison, she fled to Cuba, where President Fidel Castro granted her political asylum (Adewunmi, 2014). She remains on the FBI's Most Wanted list, with a $1,000,000 reward for her capture (Federal Bureau of Investigation, 2019). The New Jersey State Police even went so far as to say that they would consider illegally kidnapping her to take her back from Cuba (NBC News, 2017).

Fig. 61
FBI wanted poster of Assata Shakur.
Note. Source: (FBI, 2019).

Q: How did the organization come to an end?
A: The BLA argued that the government and its institutions were waging war against the Black community, which made it their duty to fight back and

wage war against the state. The organized structure of the BLA terrified law enforcement agencies. The FBI considered the BLA a national security threat and employed informants while seeking aid from other intelligence agencies. However, it was local police, especially in New York, that were most successful in combating the BLA. By 1974, law enforcement's relentless pursuit of BLA members and the capture or exile of its leaders, such as Assata Shakur, had effectively neutralized the organization. Ultimately, the police declared that the BLA problem had been resolved (Rosenau, 2013).

Q: What happened in Monroe, North Carolina, with Robert Williams?
A: In the Monroe, North Carolina area, the Ku Klux Klan organized mass rallies and carried out violence against Black communities through drive-by shootings and physical assaults. Authorities declined to intervene, allowing Klan motorcades to ride through Black neighborhoods, arguing that the terrorist Ku Klux Klan had the same constitutional right to organize as lawful Black civil rights organizations like the National Association for the Advancement of Colored People. The justice system repeatedly failed Black citizens, exemplified by the case of Louis Medlin, who attempted to rape a pregnant Black woman but was acquitted, with the judge dismissing the case using overtly racist justifications. When peaceful appeals for justice proved ineffective, Black residents felt compelled to take their defense into their own hands (Williams, 1979).

Robert F. Williams and his supporters in Monroe chose armed self-defense when the law failed to protect Black citizens from racist violence. This approach effectively deterred attacks, compelled local officials to curb Ku Klux Klan activities, and challenged the mainstream civil rights strategy of passive resistance. Their actions emphasized the significance of self-determination and survival in the face of systemic oppression (Williams, 1979).

Williams, who is a Marine Corps veteran, emphasized the right to bear arms and the need to protect Black lives when law enforcement and the courts failed to offer protection. In one instance, he described how his group created a "perimeter defense" around a house where Black civil rights workers were being attacked by White

Fig. 62
The Ku Klux Klan, a White supremacist terrorist organization, burns a cross in Florida.
Note. Source: (Associated Press, 1939).

mobs. This self-defense group used carbines, pistols, and other guns and stood their ground, scaring away the violent attackers. Williams pointed out that these actions were intended solely for defense and aimed to prevent further harm to the Black community (Williams, 1979).

Williams and his followers' acts of armed resistance transformed the way racial confrontations unfolded in Monroe. In one instance, his group responded to an attempted lynching by swiftly mobilizing and confronting the would-be attackers with weapons drawn, thereby preventing the lynching from taking place. He also recounted an episode where the police refused to intervene against a Klan motorcade that had been shooting into Black homes, prompting Williams and his men to establish roadblocks and prepare to defend the neighborhood themselves (Williams, 1979).

Q: So was Robert F. Williams punished for using weapons to defend himself and his community?
A: As a consequence of his armed self-defense activities and his outspoken stance against racial violence, Robert F. Williams faced severe backlash from both local and federal authorities. Law enforcement accused Williams of kidnapping a White couple during a civil rights protest, even though later the couple stated they had not been held against their will. In response, Williams became a fugitive and fled the United States in 1961. Initially, he sought refuge in Canada before eventually settling in Cuba, where he continued his activism and hosted a radio program denouncing American racism. The FBI pursued him as a wanted man, and his exile lasted nearly a decade before the charges were eventually dropped, allowing him to return to the U.S. in the late 1960s (Williams, 1979).

Fig. 63
Robert Williams FBI wanted poster.
Note. Source: (FBI, 1961).

Q: How did ordinary Black people resist in their everyday lives?
A: While some individuals and organizations mentioned earlier took actions that were easily noticeable, many Black people resisted oppression through small acts in their everyday lives. One example of this is the role of Black domestic workers

in the homes of White families. In these households, Black women primarily served as washerwomen, nannies, cooks, and maids, often enduring violence and abuse. Black domestic workers fought back by skipping work, stealing items from their employers, and forming informal social networks to share information about abusive employers with fellow workers (Guglielmo & Turriago, 2022).

One of the most evident forms of resistance to abusive employers was to simply quit. However, White Southern employers resented Black women's efforts to assert control over their own labor and employed coercion to maintain authority. For instance, in 1866, the Atlanta City Council enacted a law requiring employers to obtain recommendations from previous employers before hiring Black domestic workers, making it exceedingly difficult for them to find another job in the city if they left their prior position under confrontational conditions. Nonetheless, Black women persisted in resisting the exploitation by White employers by resigning from their jobs as necessary (Enobong Hannah Branch, 2011).

In the 1960s, Dorothy Bolden worked as a domestic worker. One day, the White woman who employed her told her to wash more dishes after she had completed her regular daily tasks. She refused, left her employer's house, began walking home, and, according to Bolden, was then promptly arrested by the police for talking back to a White woman. Bolden used the incident as inspiration to organize Black domestic workers by meeting with them on buses as they traveled to and from work to discuss the abuse they faced and their inadequate wages. She helped domestic workers establish a standard wage, utilize their voting power to pressure elected officials to address their needs, support Black workers in other industries who were striking, and boycott racist businesses (National Domestic Workers Alliance, 2021).

Fig. 64
Photo of a Black woman who labored in households and cotton fields.
Note. Source: (Wolcott, 1940).

Q: What role did women play in the Montgomery bus boycott that made Dr. King famous?
A: Even though Dr. Martin Luther King, Jr. is often remembered as the leader of the Montgomery bus boycott, it would have never happened without the work of Black women. One key figure was Jo Ann Gibson Robinson, the president of the Women's Political Council

(WPC). After Rosa Parks was arrested on December 1, 1955, Robinson and two students worked all night to create over 50,000 leaflets, asking people to boycott the bus for one day. Many women, traveling on foot and by car, secretly handed out these flyers around the city. When Robinson and her team found out that a group of Black ministers was meeting that Friday morning to discuss the busing situation, they took the flyers to the church, which motivated the pastors to take action. Robinson pointed out that the ministers didn't start the movement; they had to "catch up with the masses" who were already eager to act (Gibson Robinson & Garrow, 1987, pp. 1–2).

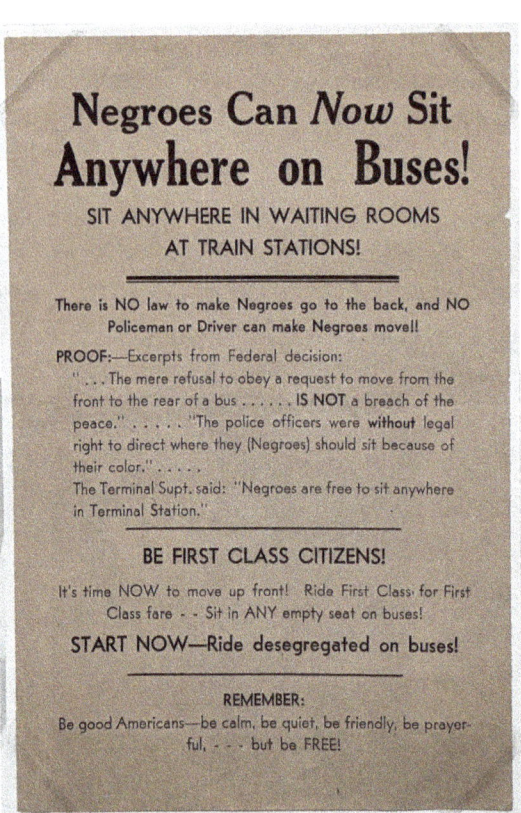

Fig. 65
Montgomery Improvement Association flyer.
Note. Source: (Montgomery Improvement Association, 1956).

Black women organized the boycott and were its backbone during its execution. Domestic workers discreetly carried news of the protest, sometimes hiding or destroying the flyers to avoid detection. One woman, however, passed the information to her White employer, and by Saturday morning, the news had reached the local press and city officials. Although the secrecy was compromised, Robinson reflected that this may have helped broaden awareness in hard-to-reach areas of the city (Gibson Robinson & Garrow, 1987). On Monday, December 5, nearly all Black riders stayed off the buses, and police escorts assigned to protect supposed "Negro goon squad" targets found little to monitor. That day, Robinson wrote, was one of unprecedented unity and dignity: "nary a colored soul" was seen riding the buses, and boycotters experienced a shared sense of pride, solidarity, and liberation (Gibson Robinson & Garrow, 1987, pp. 4–5).

Q: What role did women play in the Montgomery Improvement Association?
A: After the success of the one-day bus boycott, more than 6,000 people came to Holt Street Baptist Church on December 5, 1955, to create an organization to lead a longer bus boycott. This meeting was organized with the help of women volunteers, who handed out flyers promoting it. The

Montgomery Improvement Association (MIA) was formed and immediately began organizing the ongoing protest. Many women held significant leadership roles in the MIA. Among these women were Erna Dungee (financial secretary), Hazel Gregory (office manager), Maude Ballou (Dr. King's secretary), and Martha Johnson (secretary-clerk). Robinson and Mrs. A.W. West, Sr., were also members of the Executive Board, demonstrating that women were not only assisting the movement but also taking on leadership roles and important positions within it (Gibson, Robinson, & Garrow, 1987).

Q: How did women help financially support the Montgomery bus boycott?
A: Fundraising played a key role in the boycott's success, and women were instrumental in this effort. Georgia Gilmore started a group called the "Club from Nowhere," which raised money by selling food to both Black and White workers. Her group was soon joined by another group called "The Friendly Club," led by Inez Ricks, and they held friendly competitions to see who could raise the most money. The money they raised helped cover essential expenses, such as gas, car repairs, and purchasing vehicles for the carpool system (Gibson Robinson & Garrow, 1987).

As has often been the case, while male leaders and spokespeople received the majority of accolades, it was the determination, labor, and leadership of Black women that helped power all Black freedom movements.

> *As has often been the case, while male leaders and spokespeople received the majority of accolades, it was the determination, labor, and leadership of Black women that helped power all Black freedom movements.*

Q: How were children pivotal in the success of the Civil Rights Movement of the 1950s and 1960s?
A: Historian V.P. Franklin says that kids and teenagers played an important and often unnoticed role in the Civil Rights Movement. They were not just part of the protests; they were leaders and started many important campaigns across the country. For example, they helped integrate public schools, like the Little Rock Nine, and organized local demonstrations. Many of these young people were honor students or student leaders who volunteered to go to mostly White schools, even when they faced insulting comments and physical harm from White peers and adults. Their actions helped shape the direction

of the movement, demonstrating that the fight for justice included not just adults but also the courage and determination of Black youth (C-SPAN, 2022).

Franklin points out that young people often took action on their own without waiting for help from adults. Sometimes, teenagers were among the first to show up at marches and protests because they did not have to worry about work or financial problems that many adults faced. They were willing to get arrested, and the news coverage, especially on TV, showing kids getting hurt by police, helped push their parents and even people from around the country and the world to support them. In places like Birmingham, Alabama, and Albany, Georgia, student activists helped organize large events and highlighted the unfair treatment in segregated schools and public spaces. This grassroots activism by youth inspired others in different cities to take action when they saw their peers being arrested or harmed (C-SPAN, 2022).

Religious beliefs and institutional support played a significant role in helping young people become engaged in their communities' struggles. Many of these youth were connected to the Black church, which guided them morally and helped organize events. Churches were places where people could gather, plan protests, and prepare both spiritually and practically. Freedom Schools were established during school boycotts in cities such as Chicago and New York. These schools not only taught kids subjects like math and reading but also educated them about important political issues. They learned about the history of civil rights and the importance of fighting for them (C-SPAN, 2022).

Fig. 66
After riots in Newark, New Jersey, boarded-up and damaged buildings on a street.
Note. Source: (Leffler, 1967).

Q: In what ways did Black people collectively express their anger and frustration?
A: In the late 1960s, American racism, discrimination, segregation, and unfair treatment of Black people in the economy, politics, and society enraged Black

communities. Even after laws were passed to protect the civil and voting rights of Black people, the living conditions for many Black families did not change. In 1965, almost half of non-White people lived in poor-quality housing. Additionally, 29.1% of Black families lived in poverty, while only 7.8% of White families lived in poverty (Hine et al., 2014).

As a result, over the next few years, America's cities erupted with conflict. The most frequently discussed rebellions occurred in Watts, Los Angeles, California; Detroit, Michigan; and Newark, New Jersey. Black people, however, took to the streets and confronted police, the government, National Guard troops, and the institutions they held responsible for their poor living conditions across the nation. This is a partial list of the cities where Black people openly rebelled:

Harlem, NY 1964	New Brunswick, NJ 1967
Philadelphia, PA 1964	Buffalo, NY 1967
Rochester, NY 1964	Cincinnati, OH 1967
Watts, Los Angeles, CA 1965	Minneapolis, MN 1967
San Francisco, CA 1966	Houston, TX 1967
Dayton, OH 1966	Milwaukee, WI 1967
Cleveland, OH 1966	Chicago, IL 1968
Birmingham, AL 1967	Washington DC 1968
Boston, MA 1967	Kansas City, MO 1968
Newark, NJ 1967	Seattle, WA 1968
Detroit, MI 1967	Louisville, KY, 1968
Cambridge, MD 1967	Pittsburgh, PA 1968
Atlanta, GA 1967	Omaha, NE 1969

Q: What led to the rebellion in Plainfield, New Jersey, in 1967?
A: The causes of the rebellion in Plainfield were not unlike those in Black communities across America. The 1967 Plainfield rebellion, as described in the Kerner Commission Report, was deeply rooted in the mistreatment and systemic neglect faced by the city's Black community. By 1967, the Black population in Plainfield had reached 30%, with many residents confined to impoverished, segregated neighborhoods on the West End. This community experienced high unemployment, underemployment, and a lack of representation in government. City officials, accustomed to

managing a middle-class suburb, were described as "unprepared to handle the problems of a growing disadvantaged population" and responded to concerns from the Black community with indifference or token gestures (United States National Advisory Commission on Civil Disorders, 1968).

Access to public services in Plainfield was unequal. In 1966, for example, the city refused to build a public pool for Black youth and instead bused them to a distant county pool, charging 25 cents and requiring families to provide their own lunch, a significant burden for poor families. Educational inequality was also severe. The public schools, while technically integrated, operated under a "de facto segregation" system in which Black students were concentrated in lower academic tracks. Two-thirds of school dropouts were Black, and relations between Black students and White teachers were tense. By early 1967, even the NAACP had documented growing frustration with discrimination in housing and education, but the city council ignored these complaints (United States National Advisory Commission on Civil Disorders, 1968).

Fig. 67
The National Guard in Plainfield, New Jersey, during the 1967 rebellion.
Note. Source: (United States National Advisory Commission on Civil Disorders, 1968).

Q: How did tension between the police and Plainfield's Black community spur the 1967 rebellion?
A: Relations with the police were especially strained. Black residents viewed the police as hostile and abusive. In one incident described in the Kerner report, a woman was injured during an arrest and accused the officer of pushing her down a flight of stairs. The situation reached a flashpoint on July 14, when the same police officer was working as a private security guard at a diner. A 20-year-old Black man beat a 16-year-old Black boy bloody during an altercation, but the officer refused to get involved. When the officer refused to arrest the assailant, the community interpreted it as further proof of systemic injustice. Delegations that attempted to file formal complaints with the city were dismissed or ignored, increasing the sense that Black grievances would never be taken seriously (United States National Advisory Commission on Civil Disorders, 1968).

The flashpoint of the uprising was the police killing of Bobby Williams. According to the Kerner Commission Report, Officer John Gleason shot and wounded 22-year-old Williams, even though he was unarmed. Eyewitnesses reported that Gleason, acting alone, left his assigned post and pursued Williams into the city's West End, drew his revolver, and fired, hitting Williams, who then fled and collapsed. After the shooting, a group of local youths chased Gleason, disarmed him, and beat him to death. The youths also took his revolver, which was later reportedly used in armed resistance during the unrest. The Kerner report emphasizes that Williams "had no weapon," a fact that deepened the anger and mistrust already felt by the Black community toward the police and contributed to the intensity of the violence that followed. Frustration exploded into unrest. Youths vandalized stores and threw Molotov cocktails. Police, unprepared and undermanned, could not control the uprising (United States National Advisory Commission on Civil Disorders, 1968).

Fig. 68
The National Guard searching homes in Plainfield, New Jersey, during the 1967 rebellion.
Note. Source: (United States National Advisory Commission on Civil Disorders, 1968).

Q: What made the Plainfield rebellion different from those that happened in other cities?
A: The National Guard was called into Plainfield as it had been in Newark, where they attacked and killed Black people. Some Plainfield residents feared that the National Guard would do the same in their city. In response, some residents armed themselves in preparation for what they saw as an impending assault by state forces (United States National Advisory Commission on Civil Disorders, 1968).

The most dramatic example of this preparation occurred when Black community members organized a successful plot to steal 46 M-1 carbines from the Plainfield Machine Company, a local arms manufacturing plant (Brown, 2017). These military-grade rifles were then distributed among Black residents. The firehouse on the West End was fired upon, and several locations came under gunfire from residents who had taken up armed positions (United States National Advisory Commission on Civil Disorders, 1968).

Zayyid Muhammad, who experienced the rebellion as a young person in Plainfield, is thankful that Plainfield's Black community armed themselves, which prevented the National Guard from running roughshod over them:

> Because it was armed, our rebellion was marked by the fewest casualties of all the major rebellions during that period. And in fact, the casualties, in a real sense, were on the other side. And it's not anything to gloat about or to glorify, but it is something to appreciate (Brown, 2017).

Fig. 69
M1 Carbines.
Note. Source: (Swedish Army Museum, 2012).

This organized arming of residents marked a shift from spontaneous rioting to deliberate armed defense, driven by the belief that the violent police repression and civilian casualties that happened in Newark would happen in Plainfield. Residents also erected barricades and monitored troop movements, signaling readiness not just for protest but for armed resistance if necessary (United States National Advisory Commission on Civil Disorders, 1968). Famed revolutionary activist H. Rap Brown (a.k.a. Jamil Abdullah Al-Amin) stated:

> America has made it clear that she respects only violence. When the rebellion went down in 1967 in Plainfield, New Jersey, the cops and the National Guard came into the Black community and were raising hell until the brothers sent word that they had guns. The cops and the Guard said, hell, them niggers got guns. We can't go over there and mess with 'em (Brown, 2024).

Q: What was the most successful Black organization in America?"
A: Marcus Garvey's Universal Negro Improvement Association (UNIA) stands as the largest Black organization in history. In the early 1900s, Garvey celebrated all things Black and boldly asserted that Black was beautiful at a time when Black Americans were often taught the opposite across various

aspects of their lives (Franklin & Moss, 1998). Garvey advocated that Black people needed both a mental and physical return to Africa to be free. He held a Pan-African philosophy that viewed Black people everywhere in the world as one common people, as he explains here:

Fig. 70 Marcus Garvey, in 1924. Note. Source: (Bain News Service, 1924).

> It is for me to inform you that the Universal Negro Improvement Association is an organization that seeks to unite, into one solid body, the four hundred million Negroes in the world. To link up the fifty million Negroes in the United States of America, with the twenty million Negroes of the West Indies, the forty million Negroes of South and Central America, with the two hundred and eighty million Negroes of Africa, for the purpose of bettering our industrial, commercial, educational, social, and political conditions (Center for History and New Media Research, 2012).

By appealing to the sense of pride and dignity among Black Americans, Garvey successfully established an organization that boasted several million members (Hine et al., 2003). To this day, no other Black organization or movement has achieved the same level of membership as the UNIA. The UNIA eventually collapsed due to a combination of FBI attacks, sabotage from Garvey's political rivals, and Garvey's mismanagement of the organization's resources.

Q: Did the government of the United States really spy on and sabotage Black leaders, or is that just crazy conspiracy talk?
A: Yes, the federal government conducted both legal and illegal wiretaps on Black leaders and organizations. The FBI's surveillance of Black leaders occurred through two counterintelligence programs, COMINFIL (Communist Infiltration) and **COINTELPRO** (Counterintelligence). Domestic operatives of the FBI, known as "Division Five," executed these two programs. Until the summer of 1963, the FBI had primarily focused on performing major surveillance of Black political activists. However, after the March on Washington, the head of the FBI, J. Edgar Hoover, began to fear that Black civil rights leaders were gaining too much power and becoming a threat. Kenneth O'Reilly wrote that

> ...beginning in the summer of 1963, there was a fundamental change in Hoover's willingness to assume the risks of more aggressive involvement, a change that can be

explained by his belief that blacks had gone too far with their protests and now posed an imminent threat to the established order (O' Reilly, 1989, p. 132).

After the March on Washington, the FBI made the decision to destroy Dr. Martin Luther King, Jr. The success of the march indicated that the nation had now integrated the civil rights struggle into its national political agenda. The FBI began using every technique it had to gain damaging information on the Civil Rights Movement's most prominent spokesperson, King. By the fall of 1963, the FBI shifted from merely monitoring communist activity within the Civil Rights Movement to engaging in actual counterintelligence. The aim of the counterintelligence was to "expose, disrupt, discredit, or otherwise neutralize' the civil rights movement" (O'Reilly 1989, p.131). They wiretapped almost every location that King visited. The FBI bugged his home, the Southern Christian Leadership Conference headquarters, and numerous hotel rooms (O'Reilly, 1989). The hope was that they could uncover information that would either discredit King and the Civil Rights Movement or could be used to blackmail leaders into obedience. Despite their extensive wiretaps, the FBI never obtained enough information to significantly discredit King or the Civil Rights Movement.

Fig. 71
The founders of the Black Panther Party, Bobby Seale and Huey Newton
Note. Source: (Yanker Poster Collection, 1965).

Q: How did the FBI hinder the success of the Black Panthers?
A: The list of tactics and operations performed against the Black Panthers is so extensive that only a few examples will be cited here. The Panthers' ideology was notably different from that of most Civil Rights organizations. They were more inclined to form beliefs around Frantz Fanon's *The Wretched of the Earth* and Mao's *Little Red Book* than the Bible. They also supported militant self-defense unconditionally rather than passive non-violence. Initially, the Panthers were not on the FBI's counterintelligence target list. However, after a series of comments by Eldridge Cleaver, which included a threat to burn down the White House, beat the California Governor Ronald Reagan to death, and the production of an "off-the-pig" coloring book, they caught Hoover's attention (O'Reilly 1989).

By the end of 1968, the Black Panthers had supplanted the

Student Nonviolent Coordinating Committee (SNCC) as the FBI's primary Black threat. When Stokely Carmichael proposed that the two groups join forces, SNCC attracted the attention of the FBI once more. Division Five had no intention of allowing the Panthers to grow any stronger, and it took action to prevent the alliance from occurring. To create dissension between the two groups, it had a fictitious SNCC member call the Panthers "pinheads." Simultaneously, the FBI launched a campaign to tarnish Carmichael's reputation. They disclosed information about his sister, who married a White man of Jewish background, called his mother to warn her of a supposed assassination attempt on her son's life, and even attempted to circulate the rumor that Carmichael was a CIA informant. Although the FBI fabricated all these charges, the two organizations never fully united (O'Reilly, 1989). It was a common practice for the FBI to label members of the Panthers as informants. One COINTELPRO supervisor acknowledged that this labeling might have resulted in multiple injuries or deaths (O'Reilly 1989). Thus, the use of this tactic against Carmichael was not an isolated incident.

> *One of the FBI's most successful tactics was to pit different Black Power organizations against one another.*

The FBI continued its campaign against the Panthers by disseminating the information they acquired through wiretaps. They mailed negative information to prominent Bay Area citizens and institutions, including columnist William F. Buckley and the San Francisco Examiner. They publicized Huey Newton's upscale Oakland apartment overlooking Lake Merritt and disrupted the breakfast-for-children program by spreading a rumor that various personnel at the national headquarters of the Black Panther Party were infected with venereal disease. They also attempted to break up Panther marriages by sending letters to the wives of Panther members, claiming that their husbands had affairs with teenage girls (O'Reilly, 1989).

One of the FBI's most successful tactics was to pit different Black Power organizations against one another. In Chicago, rumors emerged that the Panthers were going to join forces with the Blackstone Rangers. The Blackstone Rangers were a collection of gangs with a history of violence, under a collective leadership called the "Main 21." The Panthers aimed to politicize the Rangers and steer Black youths away from gang activities toward community action. Even before the FBI interfered with the alliance between the two organizations, the Panthers and Rangers were struggling to unite. Several Panthers and Rangers had been involved in a shootout with each other. The FBI's meddling made an already shaky alliance even weaker. An FBI agent drafted a fictitious letter stating that the Panthers planned to kill the head of the Rangers (O'Reilly 1989). The two groups never resolved their differences and never united.

Sadly, this is only a partial listing of the attempts of the federal government to stifle Black organizations that aggressively fought for the rights of Black Americans.

Q: What other organizations did Black people form to protect and advocate for themselves?
A: Black people have resisted White America's oppression from the 1700s to the present. The following is a listing of organizations that have fought for the freedom, rights, and dignity of Black people in the United States and beyond:

18th and 19th Centuries
1. **Free African Society (1787)**
   Founded in Philadelphia by Richard Allen and Absalom Jones, this was one of the first Black mutual aid societies in the U.S., offering support to newly freed Africans and advocating for abolition and moral uplift (The Archives of the Episcopal Church, 2006).
2. **African Lodge No. 459 / Prince Hall Freemasonry (1784)**
   Founded by Prince Hall, Prince Hall Freemasons provided a base for Black mutual aid and political activism, especially in New England (Massachusetts Office of Travel and Tourism, 2024).
3. **National Negro Convention Movement**
   Between 1830 and 1900, over 600 Colored Conventions were held across North America, serving as empowering hubs for Black political thought and organizing. These gatherings, attended by prominent leaders and thousands of others, fostered community-building projects, celebrated racial unity, and protested state violence (Brown, 2016).
4. **American Moral Reform Society (1835)**
   The American Moral Reform Society aimed to uplift Black Americans and humanity through education, temperance, economy, Christian principles, and universal liberty, rejecting racial and geographic boundaries while denouncing slavery, war, and social vice (Bell, 1958).
5. **African Civilization Society (1858)**
   Founded by Henry Highland Garnet, it promoted Black emigration to Africa but also supported abolition and uplift for Black people in the U.S. (Fenner-Dorrity, 2008).

6. **National Afro-American League (1887)**
   Founded by T. Thomas Fortune, the National Afro-American League was the first national civil rights group to use litigation and state laws to fight racism, influencing later groups like the NAACP. It collapsed by the mid-1890s due to funding issues and weak national structure, but left a lasting legacy (Carle, 2015)

Fig. 72
T. Thomas Fortune
Note. Source: (American Publishing House, 1900).

Early 20th Century

7. **The National Association of Teachers in Colored Schools (1904)**
   The National Association of Teachers in Colored Schools, founded in 1904, advocated for Black teachers and students. Renamed the American Teachers Association in 1937, it merged with the National Education Association in 1966 (Lomotey, 2010).

8. **Niagara Movement (1905)**
   The Niagara Movement, founded in 1905 at Niagara Falls by prominent Black intellectuals like W.E.B. DuBois and William Monroe Trotter, was dedicated to securing civil rights for Black people. However, in 1909, facing financial constraints, many members, including DuBois, joined the newly established National Association for the Advancement of Colored People (NAACP) (Oberlin College, 2021).

9. **National Association for the Advancement of Colored People (NAACP, 1909)**
   The NAACP was founded in 1909 following the 1908 Springfield race riot in Illinois as an interracial effort to confront the increasing violence against Black people and advocate for civil and political rights. Throughout its history, the organization has played a pivotal role in landmark civil rights victories, including the 1954 *Brown v. Board of Education* Supreme Court case, and continues to be a leading voice in the fight against systemic racism and inequality (NAACP, 2025).

10. **National Urban League (1910)**
    The National Urban League, founded in 1910, is a civil rights organization dedicated to economic empowerment, equality, and social justice. With 90 affiliates, it advocates for policies and services to close the equality gap, serving over two million people annually (National Urban League, 2020).

11. **Brotherhood of Sleeping Car Porters (1925)**
    Led by A. Philip Randolph, the Brotherhood of Sleeping Car Porters (BSCP) was the first Black labor union to be recognized by a major federation, playing a crucial role in civil rights. Founded

in 1925, the BSCP fought for better working conditions and higher wages for Pullman porters, despite resistance from the Pullman Company, the American Federation of Labor, and some Black leaders. After twelve years, they secured a contract with the Pullman Company and AFL recognition, paving the way for future civil rights activism (Terrell, 2023). A. Philip Randolph also conceived the concept of a March on Washington, which was later executed by Martin Luther King, Jr. and others.

Fig. 73
A. Philip Randolph
Note. Source: (Parks, 1942).

Civil Rights Era
12. **The Congress of Racial Equality (CORE, 1942)**
    CORE's primary goal is to advocate for equality for all individuals, regardless of their race, gender, or background. CORE played a major role in the Civil Rights Movement by organizing sit-ins, the Freedom Rides, and protests against racist Jim Crow laws. Later on, CORE also worked on improving communities, making healthcare more accessible, and supporting human rights around the world by collaborating with the United Nations (Congress of Racial Equality, 2021).
13. **Southern Christian Leadership Conference (SCLC, 1957)**
    The Southern Christian Leadership Conference (SCLC) was founded in 1957 in Atlanta, Georgia, by Dr. Martin Luther King Jr. and other leaders of the Montgomery Bus Boycott. It organized major nonviolent protests, including the Birmingham Campaign, the March on Washington, and the Selma-to-Montgomery marches. These efforts contributed significantly to the passage of the Civil Rights Act of 1964 and the Voting Rights Act of 1965 (SCLC, 2024).
14. **Student Nonviolent Coordinating Committee (SNCC, 1960)**
    The Student Nonviolent Coordinating Committee (SNCC) was founded in 1960 to coordinate student-led sit-ins against segregated facilities in the South. In the early 1960s, SNCC shifted focus to voter registration in poor Black communities and organized the Mississippi Freedom Democratic Party's 1964 challenge to the all-White delegation at the Democratic National Convention. SNCC played a crucial role in major civil rights actions, such as the Selma voting rights campaign, and helped pave the way for the 1965 Voting Rights Act (Stoper, 1977).
15. **Nation of Islam (1930s–present)**
    In the 1930s, Master Wallace Fard Muhammad sought to uplift Black people by restoring their

understanding of God, self, and original identity. He appointed Elijah Muhammad as his representative, who led the movement for over four decades, promoting moral discipline, family unity, and spiritual and economic independence. The Nation teaches principles such as cleanliness, respect for women, universal peace, and the pursuit of knowledge and righteousness. Among its most notable accomplishments are its role in educating and developing figures like Malcolm X and Muhammad Ali, who became internationally renowned speakers on Black rights, and organizing the 1995 Million Man March, led by Minister Louis Farrakhan (Muhammad, 1996). While not a civil rights group in the traditional sense, the NOI's emphasis on Black self-reliance, moral reform, and racial pride provides a strong counter to anti-Black racism.

Fig. 74
Elijah Muhammad addresses followers, including Muhammad Ali
Note. Source: (Wolfson, 1964).

16. **The Organization of Afro-American Unity (OAAU, 1964)**

    The Organization of Afro-American Unity (OAAU) was established by Malcolm X following his departure from the Nation of Islam. Founded in 1964, the OAAU had four central objectives. The first goal was to re-educate Black people, fostering self-respect and a deeper understanding of their history and right to self-defense. The second objective aimed to secure political and economic power for the Black community. The third sought to forge relationships between the OAAU and Civil Rights organizations, which Malcolm X had frequently criticized during his tenure with the Nation of Islam. Finally, Malcolm X aspired for the OAAU to gain international recognition as a national liberation organization. Such recognition would enable the OAAU to present its case to the United Nations and challenge America regarding its racist practices (Sales, 1994). Tragically, Malcolm X was assassinated shortly after founding the OAAU and did not have the opportunity to help the organization achieve its goals.

Modern Organizations (1970s–Present)

17. **National Black Women's Health Project (1983)**

    The Black Women's Health Imperative (BWHI), founded in 1983 by Byllye Y. Avery, emerged from a conference at Spelman College that empowered Black women to control their health. In 1990, it opened a public education and policy office in Washington, D.C., and relocated its national headquarters there in 1995 to address racial and gender-based health disparities. Renamed in 2002, BWHI implements national programs in health policy, education, research, and leadership development, promoting the well-being of African American women and girls (Black Women's Health Imperative, 2025).

18. **Color of Change (2005)**

    Color of Change is the largest online racial justice organization in the U.S., with over 7 million members dedicated to fighting injustice and empowering Black communities. They run campaigns focused on criminal justice, media representation, voting rights, and economic equity, aiming to hold corporations and politicians accountable. Their goal is to create a world that's more humane and less hostile for Black people by transforming both the explicit and implicit rules that govern our society (Color of Change, 2025).

19. **Movement for Black Lives (2014)**

    The Movement for Black Lives (M4BL), a national network of over 150 Black-led organizations formed in 2014, strategizes and builds collective power for Black liberation. M4BL is abolitionist and anti-capitalist, advocating for the dismantling of prisons and police, and centering marginalized Black communities like trans, queer, disabled, and formerly incarcerated individuals (Movement for Black Lives, 2025).

20. **Until Freedom (2020)**

    Until Freedom is a social justice organization led by diverse people of color, dedicated to addressing systemic and racial injustice through community activism, education, and rapid response initiatives. The organization focuses on protecting lives, building wealth, and safeguarding the voting rights of people of color in underserved communities (Until Freedom, 2025).

CONCLUSION

This book began with a simple but urgent truth: if Black children do not take charge of learning their own history, they will be left vulnerable in a system that was never built to respect their humanity. Whether they attend majority-White or majority-Black schools, most Black students will be taught a version of the past that minimizes their ancestors' greatness and normalizes their oppression. They will be taught by teachers, often strangers to their culture, who unconsciously carry the weight of a negatively biased vision of who they are. And if Black children are left unarmed with knowledge, they will struggle to defend their minds, their confidence, and their futures.

This book was not written to be the end of the fight but rather its beginning. It serves as both a tool of protection and a call to action. True freedom will not come from waiting for schools to change. It will come when Black children, with the support of their families and communities, make the deliberate choice to study their history deeply, critically, and continuously. Black history is not a side note. It is the blueprint for human achievement, resilience, and brilliance. By studying it, Black children gain more than facts. They gain a foundation that no teacher, politician, or institution can ever take away.

Throughout this book, we have explored Black people's journey from the heights of African civilization to the horrors of chattel slavery and their resilience during that time. We have also highlighted their fierce determination during Reconstruction and Jim Crow, culminating in their lasting legacy of resistance and resilience in modern America. Future volumes will delve into the psychology, economics, and culture of Black life in America. However, this volume of the series intentionally focuses on lessons that expose this truth: Black history did not start in chains, nor is it a mere footnote to the history of others. It is the foundation of human civilization and the ongoing human struggle for freedom and dignity.

Michaela Angemeer wrote, "You cannot use someone else's map to find yourself." I hope that this book will help Black children discover their true selves and the paths they must take to realize their fullest potential, both for themselves and for their people.

Glossary

Abolitionist – A person who actively worked to end slavery, especially during the 18th and 19th centuries.

Afro-Latinos – People of both African and Latin American heritage, often part of the African diaspora in Latin America.

Anti-capitalist – Someone who opposes capitalism and its focus on private profit, often in favor of more equitable systems.

Auctioneer – A person who ran public sales, including those where enslaved people were sold.

Capitalism – An economic system where individuals or corporations own businesses and aim to make profits.

Casualties – People who are killed, wounded, or go missing during wars or violent events.

Chattel – Movable personal property; under slavery, it meant enslaved people were treated as property, not humans.

Civilization – A society that develops beyond merely meeting its necessities for survival and engages in art, law, and philosophical reflection.

Colonialism – The domination and exploitation of one region or people by another, often for economic gain.

Commodity – A valuable good that can be bought or sold; enslaved people were treated as commodities during slavery.

Dehumanization – Treating people as less than human to justify abuse or violence.

Diaspora – The forced movement of a population from their homeland, resulting in a people being spread out across the world, such as the African diaspora due to slavery.

Dynasty – A series of rulers from the same family, common in ancient societies.

Empire – A large territory or group of territories controlled by a single ruler or power.

Enslaved – A person forced into slavery, denied freedom, and treated as property.

Eurocentric – Viewing history or the world mainly from a European point of view.

Genocide – The intentional destruction of a group of people based on race, ethnicity, or nationality.

Ideology – A set of ideas or beliefs that guide political or social actions.

Indigenous – The first people to live in a region, often affected by colonization.

Inoculation – A method used to protect people from diseases by exposing them to a small, controlled amount.

Institutional – Related to systems like governments or schools, especially when describing racism or injustice built into them.

Intercommunalism – A theory encouraging oppressed communities to work together across race or geography to fight injustice.

Jim Crow – A set of laws in the southern U.S. that enforced racial segregation after the Civil War.

Ku Klux Klan – A White supremacist hate group in the United States that has used violence and terror to try to keep Black people and other minority groups from having equal rights.

Middle Passage – The brutal journey across the Atlantic Ocean that enslaved Africans were forced to endure.

Monotheism – The belief in only one god.

NAACP (National Association for the Advancement of Colored People) – A civil rights organization founded in 1909 to fight against racism and segregation and to ensure equal rights for Black Americans.

Oppression – Prolonged, unjust treatment of people by those in power.

Persecution – Harsh or violent treatment of people because of their beliefs, race, or identity.

Psychological – Related to the mind; includes mental suffering, especially in the context of slavery and trauma.

Rebellion – An organized effort to fight back against authority or oppression.

Resilience – The ability to recover from hardship, oppression, or trauma.

Resistance – Acts of opposition to power or injustice, such as revolts or protests.

Segregated – Separated by law or practice, often by race.

Segregation – The practice of keeping racial groups apart, especially in public spaces and schools.

Slavers – People involved in capturing, selling, or transporting enslaved people.

Slavery – A system where people are owned as property and forced to work without rights.

Speculum – A tool used by doctors, misused on enslaved Africans to force-feed them.

Systemic oppression – Unfair treatment and discrimination built into the laws, rules, and practices of a society, making it harder for certain groups to succeed.

Urbanization – The growth and development of cities as people move from rural areas.

References

The Archives of the Episcopal Church. (2006). *The church awakens: African Americans and the struggle for justice*. Episcopalarchives.org. https://episcopalarchives.org/church-awakens/exhibits/show/legacy/free-african-society

16th Street Baptist Church. (n.d.). *Book a tour of 16th Street Baptist Church and see history for yourself!* 16th Street Baptist Church. Retrieved May 26, 2025, from https://www.16thstreetbaptist.org/tours/

Abraham Lincoln Presidential Library and Museum. (2024). *Examining Lincoln's Views On African Americans And Slavery*. Abraham Lincoln Presidential Library and Museum. https://presidentlincoln.illinois.gov/learn/educators/educator-resources/teaching-guides/lincolns-views-african-american-slavery/#:~:text=I%20am%20not%2C%20nor%20ever

Adewunmi, B. (2014, July 13). *Assata Shakur: from civil rights activist to FBI's most-wanted*. The Guardian. https://www.theguardian.com/books/2014/jul/13/assata-shakur-civil-rights-activist-fbi-most-wanted

Africa - People | Britannica. (2019). In *Encyclopædia Britannica*. https://www.britannica.com/place/Africa/People

Alabama Department of Archives and History. (2021). Poll Tax receipt for Rosa Boyles of Jefferson County, Alabama, October 22, 1920 [Online image]. In *Wikimedia Commons*. https://commons.wikimedia.org/wiki/File:Poll_Tax_receipt_for_Rosa_Boyles_of_Jefferson_County,_Alabama,_October_22,_1920.png

Allen, J. (2000). Without sanctuary : lynching photography in America. Twin Palms.

Allers, K. S. (2019, March 21). Perspective | The tough choices black parents face when choosing a school for their children. *Washington Post*. https://www.washingtonpost.com/lifestyle/2019/03/25/head-or-heart-black-parents-face-tough-trade-offs-when-it-comes-education/

Allyn, N. (2024). *Nat Turner's Rebellion, 1831 A Spotlight on a Primary Source*. History Resources; The Gilder Lehrman Institute of American History. https://www.gilderlehrman.org/history-resources/spotlight-primary-source/nat-turner%E2%80%99s-rebellion-1831

American Publishing House. (1900). Timothy Thomas Fortune circa 1900 [Online image]. In *Wikimedia Commons*. https://commons.wikimedia.org/wiki/File:T._Thomas_Fortune.jpg

anatolikFOTO. (2024). A man's crooked teeth. Young man showing crooked growing teeth. In *Envato*. https://elements.envato.com/a-mans-crooked-teeth-young-man-showing-crooked-gro-CK9JWGT

Anderson, C. (1994). *Black Labor, White Wealth*. Powernomics Corporation of America.

Anderson, C. (2016). *White Rage: The Unspoken Truth of Our Racial Divide* (Kindle). Bloomsbury, An Imprint Of Bloomsbury Publishing Plc.

Anderson, J. (2011). A Tension in the Political Thought of Huey P. Newton. *Journal of African American Studies*, 16(2), 249–267. https://doi.org/10.1007/s12111-011-9207-9

Anderson, S. E., Holley, V., & Cro-Maat Collective. (1995). *The black holocaust for beginners*. For Beginners ; London.

Anderson, T. (1993). Introduction to African American Studies. Kendall Hunt.

Ani, M. (1994). Let the Circle be Unbroken. Red Sea Press(NJ).

Antrim, Z. (1999). *Wonders of the African World - Episodes - Slave Kingdoms*. Www.pbs.org. https://www.pbs.org/wonders/Episodes/Epi3/slave_2.htm

Aptheker, H. (2013). American Negro slave revolts. International Publishers.

Associated Press. (1939). Members of the Ku Klux Klan, wearing traditional white hoods and robes, stand back and watch with their arms crossed after burning a 15-foot cross at Tampa, Fla., Jan. 30, 1939. In *Wikimedia Commons*. https://commons.wikimedia.org/wiki/File:Ku_Klux_Klan_demonstration_in_Tampa.jpg

Authentic and Impartial Narrative of the Tragical Scene Which Was Witnessed in Southampton County. (2007). Nat Turner woodcut [Online image]. In *Wikimedia Commons*. https://commons.wikimedia.org/wiki/File:Nat_Turner_woodcut.jpg

Axelrod, J., & Faulkner, J. (2019, October 24). *Tulane cannot ignore its historical roots to slavery • The Tulane Hullabaloo*. The Tulane Hullabaloo; The Hullabaloo. https://tulanehullabaloo.com/50267/views/tulane-cannot-ignore-its-historical-roots-to-slavery/

Bain News Service. (1924). Marcus Garvey in August 1924 [Online image]. In *Wikimedia Commons*. https://commons.wikimedia.org/wiki/File:Marcus_Garvey_1924-08-05.jpg

Baptist, E. E. (2015, August 24). *An Essential Tool That Fueled the Cotton Industry's Explosive Growth. (It's Not the Cotton Gin.)*. Slate Magazine. https://slate.com/human-interest/2015/08/slavery-under-the-pushing-system-why-systematic-violence-became-a-necessity.html

Barnett. (2015). Ida-b-wells-barnett1 [Online image]. In *Wikimedia Commons*. https://commons.wikimedia.org/wiki/File:Ida-b-wells-barnett1.jpg

Barragan, Y. (2017, June 26). *Uncovering Lisbon's Forgotten History of Slavery - AAIHS*. Www.aaihs.org. https://www.aaihs.org/uncovering-lisbons-forgotten-history-of-slavery/#:~:text=Sometime%20between%201441%20and%201444

Bates, M., McGann, K., & Quinn, V. (Directors). (2017). *Africa's Great Civilizations*. PBS.

BBC News Africa. (2020). *Cattle, Crops and Iron - History Of Africa with Zeinab Badawi [Episode 2]*. Www.youtube.com; BBC News Africa. https://youtu.be/Srlf_xltWfc?si=8lAEPWT2noRt3PWm

Beatty, I. (2006). San tribesman [Online image]. In *Wikimedia Commons*. https://commons.wikimedia.org/wiki/File:San_tribesman.jpg

Beckert , S., & Desan, C. (2018). American Capitalism : New Histories. Columbia University Press.

Bell, H. H. (1958). The American Moral Reform Society, 1836-1841. *The Journal of Negro Education*, *27*(1), 34. https://doi.org/10.2307/2293690

Bennett, L. (2000). Forced into glory : Abraham Lincoln's white dream. Johnson Pub. Co.

Berlin, I. (2006). Slaves no more : three essays on emancipation and the Civil War. Cambridge Cambridge Univ. Press.

Berlin, I., & WGBH Educational Foundation. (2024). *Historian Ira Berlin | American Experience | PBS*. Www.pbs.org; WGBH Educational Foundation. https://www.pbs.org/wgbh/americanexperience/features/lincolns-berlin/#:~:text=On%20the%20eve%20of%20the%20Civil%20War%20slightly%20more%20than

Berry, D. R. (2011, October 31). *Daina Ramey Berry on Slavery, Work and Sexuality*. Not Even Past. https://notevenpast.org/daina-ramey-berry-slavery-work-and-sexuality/

Berry, D. R. (2018, March 6). *176 Daina Ramey Berry, The Value of the Enslaved From Womb to Grave* (L. Covart, Interviewer) [Interview]. https://youtu.be/r4KUYkK53L4?si=5axKQBdZC1fhbvDL

Bicks, M., & Strachan, A. L. (2022). Riveted: The History of Jeans. In *PBS*. https://www.pbs.org/video/riveted-the-history-of-jeans-giam2l/

Black Liberation Army. (1970). Logo of the Black Liberation Army, an American far-left black nationalist group which splintered from the Black Panther Party [Online Image]. In *Wikimedia Commons*. https://commons.wikimedia.org/wiki/File:Black_Liberation_Army_logo.svg

Black Panther Party Alumni Legacy Network. (2025). *Black Panther Party Alumni Legacy Network*. Black Panther Party Alumni Legacy Network. https://bppaln.org/programs?utm_source=chatgpt.com

Black Panthers. (1966, October 15). *Black Panther's Ten-Point Program*. Marxists.org. https://www.marxists.org/history/usa/workers/black-panthers/1966/10/15.htm

Black Women's Health Imperative. (2025). *Our Story*. Black Women's Health Imperative. https://bwhi.org/our-story/

Blassingame, J. W. (1979). *The slave community*. Oxford University Press.

Blatch, S. (2013, February 1). *Great achievements in science and technology in ancient Africa*. Www.asbmb.org. https://www.asbmb.org/asbmb-today/science/020113/great-achievements-in-stem-in-ancient-africa

Blight, D., Frey, S., Nash, G., & Wood, P. (2019). Africans in America/Part 1/Living Africans Thrown Overboard. Pbs.org. https://www.pbs.org/wgbh/aia/part1/1h280.html

Boissoneault, L. (2018, September 28). *The Deadliest Massacre in Reconstruction-Era Louisiana Happened 150 Years Ago*. Smithsonian Magazine. https://www.smithsonianmag.com/history/story-deadliest-massacre-reconstruction-era-louisiana-180970420/

Boustan, L. (2018, June 1). *The Great Black Migration: Opportunity and competition in Northern labor markets*. INSTITUTE for RESEARCH on POVERTY. https://www.irp.wisc.edu/resource/the-great-black-migration-opportunity-and-competition-in-northern-labor-markets/

Brady , M. B., & Handy, L. C. (2006). P. B. S. Pinchback - Brady-Handy [Online image]. In *Wikimedia Commons*. https://commons.wikimedia.org/wiki/File:P._B._S._Pinchback_-_Brady-Handy.jpg

Brady, M. B. (1863). Cicatrices de flagellation sur un esclave [Online image]. In *Wikimedia Commons*. https://commons.wikimedia.org/wiki/File:Cicatrices_de_flagellation_sur_un_esclave.jpg

Brians, P. (2016, November 4). *Leo Africanus: Description of Timbuktu from the description of Africa (1526)*. Leo Africanus: Description of Timbuktu from the Description of Africa (1526). https://brians.wsu.edu/2016/11/04/leo-africanus-description-of-timbuktu-from-the-description-of-africa-1526/

Brice, A. (2020, February 11). *The Montgomery bus boycott and the women who made it possible*. Berkeley News. https://news.berkeley.edu/2020/02/11/podcast-montgomery-bus-boycott-womens-political-council/

Brito, L. (2022, June 17). *Portraits of Black Politics and Resistance in Brazil*. NACLA. https://nacla.org/black-politics-resistance-brazil#:~:text=Over%20half%20of%20the%20nation

Browder, A. T. (2007). Nile valley contributions to civilization. Unknown Inst Of Karmic Guidance.

Brown University. (2017, August 2). *Evening Talk with Sowande' Mustakeem*. YouTube. https://youtu.be/SKw28dAYPz8?si=h2-L5NwYWN3jguKH

Brown University. (2021). *Brown's Slavery & Justice Report, Digital 2nd Edition | Brown University*. Brown's Slavery & Justice Report, Digital 2nd Edition | Brown University. https://slaveryandjusticereport.brown.edu

Brown, A. (Director). (2017). Voices of a Rebellion: Plainfield, New Jersey 1967 [Film]. Alrick Brown.

Brown, E. (2016). *The meeting that launched a movement: The first national convention*. The Colored Conventions Project. https://coloredconventions.org/about-conventions/

Brown, H. R. (2024). *Die Nigger Die: A Political Autobiography* . Historyisaweapon.com; History is a Weapon. https://www.historyisaweapon.com/defcon1/dnd.html

Buckley, K., Weaver, B., West, V., & Shaw, J. (2024). Overview · The History of Enslaved People at UA, 1828-1865 · The History of Enslaved People at UA. Studyingslavery.ua.edu. https://studyingslavery.ua.edu/s/uastudyingslavery/page/overview

Burnett, J. (2021, February 28). *A Chapter In U.S. History Often Ignored: The Flight Of Runaway Slaves To Mexico*. NPR.org. https://www.npr.org/2021/02/28/971325620/a-chapter-in-u-s-history-often-ignored-the-flight-of-runaway-slaves-to-mexico

Buttre, J. C. (1855). Frederick Douglass as a younger man [Online image]. In *Wikimedia Commons*. https://commons.wikimedia.org/wiki/File:Frederick_Douglass_as_a_younger_man.jpg

C-SPAN. (2022, February 22). *V.P. Franklin*. C-SPAN.org; C-SPAN. https://www.c-span.org/program/qa/vp-franklin/608760

Carle, S. D. (2015). Defining the struggle : National organizing for racial justice, 1880-1915. Oxford University Press.

Cartwright, S. (2019). *Africans in America/Part 4/"Diseases and Peculiarities."* Pbs.org. https://www.pbs.org/wgbh/aia/part4/4h3106t.html

Center for History and New Media Research. (2012). "If You Believe the Negro Has a Soul": "Back to Africa" with Marcus Garvey. Historymatters.gmu.edu. https://historymatters.gmu.edu/d/5124/

Chafe, W. H., Gavins, R., & Korstad, R. (2001). *Remembering Jim Crow*. New Press, The.

Charlotte Forten Grimké full. (2013). [Online image]. In *Wikimedia Commons*. https://commons.wikimedia.org/wiki/File:Charlotte_Forten_Grimk%C3%A9_full.jpg

Chicago Defender. (1920). Scott and Violet Srthur arrive with their family at Chicago's Polk Street depot on Aug. 30, 1920, two months after their two sons were lynched in Paris, Texas. [Online image]. In *Wikimedia Commons*. https://commons.wikimedia.org/wiki/File:Great_migration.jpg

Chinguwo, P. G. (2008). Mali: The Wonders of Dogon Astronomy . *New African* , (London. 1978), 2008-04 (472), p., 44–45.

Clark, A. (2018, August 26). *How "The Birth of a Nation" Revived the Ku Klux Klan*. HISTORY. https://www.history.com/news/kkk-birth-of-a-nation-film

Clark, A. (2022, January 4). *How Southern Landowners Tried to Restrict the Great Migration.* HISTORY. https://www.history.com/news/great-migration-southern-landowners

Clay, E. W. (2008). Jimcrow [Online image]. In *Wikimedia Commons.* https://commons.wikimedia.org/wiki/File:Jimcrow.jpg

Clayman Institute for Gender Research. (2014, January 6). *Women were key in the Black Panther Party | The Clayman Institute for Gender Research.* Gender.stanford.edu; Stanford University. https://gender.stanford.edu/news/women-were-key-black-panther-party

CNN, D. (2018, July 27). *Stepping through Ghana's "Door of No Return."* CNN. https://www.cnn.com/2018/07/27/africa/ghana-elmina-castle/index.html

Coker, R. (2011, September 21). *Historian Revises Estimate of Civil War Dead.* Binghamton University Research News. https://discovere.binghamton.edu/news/civilwar-3826.html

Collection of the Smithsonian National Museum of African American History and Culture. (1972). Flier picturing and promoting the Black Panther Party free food program, specifically at the black community survival conference. [Online image]. In *Wikimedia Commons.* https://commons.wikimedia.org/wiki/File:Flier_for_the_Black_Community_Survival_Conference.jpg

Color of Change. (2025). Color Of Change helps you do something real about injustice. Colorofchange.org. https://colorofchange.org/about/

Columbia University. (2014). *Did You Know… | Columbia University Libraries.* Columbiaandslavery.columbia.edu; Columbia University Department of History. https://columbiaandslavery.columbia.edu/about/did-you-know.html

Congress of Racial Equality. (2021). *CORE Facts.* Congress of Racial Equality. https://www.thecongressofracialequality.org/core-facts.html

Coordinating Committee: The Black Liberation Army. (1976). A message to the black movment: a political statement from the black underground. In *MSU Libraries.* Michigan State University Libraries. https://archive.lib.msu.edu/DMC/AmRad/messageblackmovement.pdf

Cotterell, B., Dickson, F. P., & Kamminga, J. (1986). Ancient Egyptian water-clocks: A reappraisal. *Journal of Archaeological Science, 13*(1), 31–50.

Cox, J. (2002, February 21). *USATODAY.com - Corporations challenged by reparations activists.* Usatoday30.Usatoday.com. http://usatoday30.usatoday.com/money/general/2002/02/21/slave-reparations.htm

Cresques, A. (2023). Catalan Atlas BNF Sheet 6 Mansa Musa (cropped) [Online image]. In *Wikimedia Commons.* https://commons.wikimedia.org/wiki/File:Catalan_Atlas_BNF_Sheet_6_Mansa_Musa_(cropped).jpg

Crisis. (2009). Postcard of the lynched Will Stanley front and back [Online image]. In *Wikimedia*. https://commons.wikimedia.org/wiki/File:Postcard_of_the_lynched_Will_Stanley_front_and_back.jpg

Daily Worker. (2024). Recy Taylor (1944) [Online image]. In *Wikimedia Commons*. https://commons.wikimedia.org/wiki/File:Recy_Taylor_(1944).png

Danzer, G. A., de Alva , J. J. L., Krieger, L. S., Wilson, L. E., & Woloch, N. (2002). *The Americans Grades 9-12*. McDougal Littell/Houghton Mifflin.

Dartmouth & Slavery Project. (2024). *Dartmouth & Slavery Project | Dartmouth Libraries*. Www.library.dartmouth.edu; Dartmouth College. https://www.library.dartmouth.edu/slavery-project

Davidson, B. (2004). The African slave trade. Oxford Currey.

Delano, J. (1942). Photo of child with newspaper [Online image]. In *Wikimedia Commons*. https://commons.wikimedia.org/wiki/File:Child_selling_Chicago_Tribune.jpg

Delano, J. (1944). Group of Florida migrants near Shawboro, North Carolina on their way to Cranberry, New Jersey, to pick potatoes. [Online Image]. In *Wikimedia Commons*. https://commons.wikimedia.org/wiki/File:Migrant_Workers_July_1940_from_Florida_to_New_Jersey.jpg

Department of History, University of Pennsylvania. (2022, October 19). A Bare and Open Truth The Penn and Slavery Project and the Public (VanJessica Gladney – PERSPECTIVES) | Penn Arts & Sciences Department of History. Live-Sas-Www-History.pantheon.sas.upenn.edu. https://live-sas-www-history.pantheon.sas.upenn.edu/node/14902

Desmond, M. (2019, August 14). American Capitalism Is Brutal. You Can Trace That to the Plantation. *The New York Times*. https://www.nytimes.com/interactive/2019/08/14/magazine/slavery-capitalism.html

Dibrova. (2024). The White House. In *Envato Elements*. https://elements.envato.com/the-white-house-P6TLL3N

Diliff. (2007). St Peter's Square, Vatican City - April 2007 [Online image]. In *Wikimedia Commons*. https://commons.wikimedia.org/wiki/File:St_Peter%27s_Square,_Vatican_City_-_April_2007.jpg

Dotinga, R. (2015, July 8). *The famous 1861 "Cornerstone Speech" that aimed for hard truths about the Confederate battle flag*. The Christian Science Monitor; The Christian Science Monitor. https://www.csmonitor.com/Books/chapter-and-verse/2015/0708/The-famous-1861-Cornerstone-Speech-that-aimed-for-hard-truths-about-the-Confederate-battle-flag

Douglas, E. (1965). Wherever death may surprise us, it will be welcome, provided that this, our battle cry, reach some receptive ear ... In *Library of Congress*. https://www.loc.gov/item/2015649358/

Douglass, F. (1845). Narrative of the Life of Frederick Douglass. Clydesdale Press.

Dray, P. (2007). At the Hands of Persons Unknown : the Lynching of Black America. Random House Publishing Group.

Dunham, W. (2024, March 26). *Researchers finally reveal where the first humans went after leaving Africa*. The Independent. https://www.independent.co.uk/news/science/archaeology/homo-sapiens-africa-italy-europe-b2518760.html

Editors of Encyclopedia Britannica. (2017). Timbuktu | Mali. In *Encyclopædia Britannica*. https://www.britannica.com/place/Timbuktu-Mali

Eleftheriou-Smith, L.-M. (2015, April 7). *How Europeans got their white skin*. The Independent. https://www.independent.co.uk/news/science/how-europeans-evolved-to-have-white-skin-starting-from-around-8-000-years-ago-10160120.html

Encyclopedia Virginia. (2020, December 7). *An act to amend the act concerning slaves, free negroes and mulattoes (April 7, 1831) - Encyclopedia Virginia*. Encyclopedia Virginia; Encyclopedia Virginia. https://encyclopediavirginia.org/primary-documents/an-act-to-amend-the-act-concerning-slaves-free-negroes-and-mulattoes-april-7-1831/

Enobong Hannah Branch. (2011). Opportunity denied : Limiting Black women to devalued work (pp. 49–70). Rutgers University Press.

Environment, U. N. (2017, October 25). *Our work in Africa*. UNEP - UN Environment Programme. https://www.unep.org/regions/africa/our-work-africa

Equal Justice Initiative. (2022). *Origins: The Transatlantic slave trade*. Equal Justice Initiative Reports; The Equal Justice Initiative. https://eji.org/report/transatlantic-slave-trade/origins/#the-barbarity-of-the-middle-passage

European Commission. (2022, September 23). *New archaeology dives into the mysterious demise of the Neanderthals | Research and Innovation*. Projects.research-And-Innovation.ec.europa.eu. https://projects.research-and-innovation.ec.europa.eu/en/horizon-magazine/new-archaeology-dives-mysterious-demise-neanderthals

Evanzz, K. (1999). The messenger : the rise and fall of Elijah Muhammad. Vintage Books.

Farnum, G. H. (2011). Laura Nelson high res [Online image]. In *Wikimedia Commons*. https://commons.wikimedia.org/wiki/File:Laura_Nelson_high_res.jpg

FBI. (1961). FBI "wanted" flyer for civil rights activist Robert F. Williams [Online image]. In *Wikimedia Commons*. https://commons.wikimedia.org/wiki/File:Hooverwarrantforwilliams.jpg

FBI. (1970). Photo from FBI file Los Angeles, [California] [Online Image]. In *U.S. National Archives*. https://www.archives.gov/research/african-americans/individuals/elaine-brown?utm_source=chatgpt.com

FBI. (2019). Most wanted terrorist. In *FBI*. https://www.fbi.gov/wanted/wanted_terrorists/joanne-deborah-chesimard/download.pdf

Federal Bureau of Investigation. (2019). *Joanne Deborah Chesimard*. Federal Bureau of Investigation; Federal Bureau of Investigation. https://www.fbi.gov/wanted/wanted_terrorists/joanne-deborah-chesimard

Fenner-Dorrity, E. (2008, November 19). *The African Civilization Society (1858-1869)* •. Black Past; www.blackpast.org. https://www.blackpast.org/global-african-history/african-civilization-society-1858-1869/

Fleischer, M. (2019, December 8). *50 years ago, SWAT raided the L.A. Black Panthers. It's been targeting Black communities ever since*. Los Angeles Times. https://www.latimes.com/opinion/story/2019-12-08/50-years-swat-black-panthers-militarized-policinglos-angeles

Fling, S. (2024). *Enslaved Labor and the Construction of the U.S. Capitol*. WHHA (En-US). https://www.whitehousehistory.org/enslaved-labor-and-the-construction-of-the-u-s-capitol

Foner, E. (1988). Reconstruction : America's unfinished revolution, 1863-1877. Harper & Row.

Foner, E. (1990). A Short History of Reconstruction, 1863-1877. HarperCollins Publishers.

Fortin, J. (2018, October 13). U.N.C. Chancellor Apologizes for History of Slavery at Chapel Hill. *The New York Times*. https://www.nytimes.com/2018/10/13/us/unc-carolina-apologize-slavery.html

Franke-Ruta, G. (2011, February 21). *How "Washington" Became the Blackest Name in America*. The Atlantic. https://www.theatlantic.com/politics/archive/2011/02/how-washington-became-the-blackest-name-in-america/71511/#

Franklin, J. H., & Moss, A. A. (1998). From slavery to freedom : a history of African Americans. Vol. 2. Mcgraw-Hill.

Garcia-Moreno, O. (2017). Gold deposits in West Africa showing historical and current mining activity [Online image]. In *Wikimedia Commons*. https://commons.wikimedia.org/wiki/File:West_African_Gold_Fields.png#Licensing

Gates, Jr., H. L. (2013, January 18). *Why Did Free Blacks Stay in the South? African American History Blog | The African Americans: Many Rivers to Cross*. The African Americans: Many Rivers to

Cross; WNET. https://www.pbs.org/wnet/african-americans-many-rivers-to-cross/history/free-blacks-lived-in-the-north-right/

Gates, H. L. (1987). The classic slave narratives. Signet Classics.

Georgetown University. (2024). *Georgetown Reflects on Slavery, Memory, and Reconciliation*. Georgetown University. https://www.georgetown.edu/slavery/

Ghose, T. (2014, January 27). *7,000-year-old human bones suggest new date for light-skin gene*. Www.cbsnews.com. https://www.cbsnews.com/news/7000-year-old-human-bones-suggest-new-date-for-light-skin-gene/

Gibson Robinson, J. A., & Garrow, D. (1987). Montgomery Bus Boycott and the women who started it: The Memoir of Jo Ann Gibson Robinson. In *National Humanities Center Resource Toolbox*. https://nationalhumanitiescenter.org/pds/maai3/protest/text5/robinsonbusboycott.pdf

Gildersleeve, F. (2018). Lynching of Jesse Washington, 1916 [Online image]. In *Wikimedia Commons*. https://commons.wikimedia.org/wiki/File:Lynching_of_Jesse_Washington,_1916_(cropped).jpg

Gilmore, G. E. (1996). Gender and Jim Crow : women and the politics of white supremacy in North Carolina, 1896-1920. University Of North Carolina Press.

Gomez, F., Hirbo, J., & Tishkoff, S. A. (2014). Genetic Variation and Adaptation in Africa: Implications for Human Evolution and Disease. *Cold Spring Harbor Perspectives in Biology, 6*(7), a008524–a008524. https://doi.org/10.1101/cshperspect.a008524

Google Arts & Culture Experiments. (2024, June 7). *The Timbuktu Manuscripts*. Google Arts & Culture. https://artsandculture.google.com/experiment/the-timbuktu-manuscripts/BQE6pL2U3Qsu2A?hl=en

Gross, T. (2017, May 3). *A "Forgotten History" Of How The U.S. Government Segregated America*. NPR. https://www.npr.org/2017/05/03/526655831/a-forgotten-history-of-how-the-u-s-government-segregated-america

Guglielmo, J., & Turriago, N. (2022). dwherstories.com. A History of Domestic Work and Worker Organizing. https://www.dwherstories.com/timeline/survival-perseverance-and-resistance

Hallam, J. (2019). *Slavery and the Making of America . The Slave Experience: The Family | PBS*. Thirteen.org. https://www.thirteen.org/wnet/slavery/experience/family/history2.html

Harper's Weekly. (1873). The Louisiana murders—gathering the dead and wounded [Online image]. In *Wikimedia Commons*. https://commons.wikimedia.org/wiki/File:ColfaxMassacre.jpg

Harris Dixon, J. (2019, March 4). *The Rank and File Women of the Black Panther Party and Their Powerful Influence*. Smithsonian Magazine; Smithsonian Magazine. https://

www.smithsonianmag.com/smithsonian-institution/rank-and-file-women-black-panther-party-their-powerful-influence-180971591/

Harris, P. (2012, June 16). *How the end of slavery led to starvation and death for millions of black Americans*. The Guardian; The Guardian. https://www.theguardian.com/world/2012/jun/16/slavery-starvation-civil-war

Hays, B. (2017, May 8). *Modern DNA reveals ancient origins of Indian population*. UPI. https://www.upi.com/Science_News/2017/05/08/Modern-DNA-reveals-ancient-origins-of-Indian-population/6721494272565/

Hebbard, J. (2022, August 22). *New Digital Resource on the History of Slavery at UGA | UGA Libraries*. Www.libs.uga.edu; University of Georgia. https://www.libs.uga.edu/news/new-digital-resource-history-slavery-uga

Henshilwood, C. S. (2014). Blombo [Online image]. In *Wikimedia Commons.* https://commons.wikimedia.org/wiki/File:Blombo.jpg

Hicks, T., & Grozelier, L. (1860). Thomas Hicks - Leopold Grozelier - Presidential candidate Abraham Lincoln 1860 - cropped to lithographic plate [Online image]. In *Wikimedia Commons.* https://commons.wikimedia.org/wiki/File:Thomas_Hicks_-_Leopold_Grozelier_-_Presidential_Candidate_Abraham_Lincoln_1860_-_cropped_to_lithographic_plate.jpg

Hilliard, A. G. (1992). The meaning of KMT (ancient egyptian) history for contemporary african american experience. *Phylon (1960-)*, 49, 1/2. http://www.jstor.org/stable/3132613

Hine, D. C., Hine, W. C., & Harrold, S. (2014). *African Americans : a concise history*. Pearson.

History on the Net. (2014, May 27). *Black Peoples of America - The Slave Auction*. History on the Net. https://www.historyonthenet.com/black-peoples-of-america-the-slave-auction#:~:text=The%20auctioneer%20would%20decide%20a

History.com. (2022, December 14). *Loving v. Virginia: 1967 & Supreme Court Case - HISTORY*. History.com; History.com. https://www.history.com/topics/black-history/loving-v-virginia#supreme-court-ruling

History.com. (2023, November 3). *Life Aboard a Slave Ship*. Www.history.com; History.com. https://www.history.com/topics/slavery/life-aboard-a-slave-ship-video

Hodgson, P. (2020, March 3). *Shareholder seeks reparations for slave-built railroad*. Responsible Investor. https://www.responsible-investor.com/shareholder-seeks-reparations-for-slave-built-railroad/

Holloway, J. E. (2005). Africanisms in American culture. Indiana University Press.

Horn, C. (2017, November 30). *History unveiled: Ceremony dedicates historical markers acknowledging enslaved workers*. University of South Carolina; University of South Carolina. https://sc.edu/uofsc/posts/2017/12/history_unveiled.php

Hughes, G. (2022, July 21). *Ida B. Wells Famous Quotes*. Historic Newspapers. https://www.historic-newspapers.com/blog/ida-b-wells-quotes/

Hunter, T. W. (2019, September 20). *Married Slaves Faced Wrenching Separations, or Even Choosing Family Over Freedom*. HISTORY. https://www.history.com/news/african-american-slavery-marriage-family-separation

Hurmence, B. (2005). *My Folks Don't Want Me to Talk about Slavery*. John F. Blair, Publisher. (Original work published 1984)

Illustrated London News. (1861). A Slave Auction in Virginia ILN-1861-0216-0005 [Online image]. In *Wikimedia Commons*.

Jablonka, I. (2019). *On Board The Slave Ship*. Booksandideas.net. https://booksandideas.net/On-Board-The-Slave-Ship

Jacobs, H. A., & Douglass, F. (2011). Incidents in the life of a slave girl & Narrative of the life of Frederick Douglass : two memoirs of notable African-Americans during the nineteenth century. Leonaur, An Imprint Of Oakpast, Ltd.

James, D. J., Pellett, G., Gazit, C., & Farrell, L. D. (2004). Slavery and the Making of America - Episode 4 [DVD]. In *Thirteen*.

Johnson, J. W. (1917). *Lift every voice and sing*. https://poets.org/poem/lift-every-voice-and-sing

Jolly, J. (2020, June 18). *Barclays, HSBC and Lloyds among UK banks that had links to slavery*. The Guardian. https://www.theguardian.com/business/2020/jun/18/barclays-hsbc-and-lloyds-among-uk-banks-that-had-links-to-slavery

Jolly, J. (2022, April 15). *Bank of England owned 599 slaves in 1770s, new exhibition reveals*. The Guardian. https://www.theguardian.com/world/2022/apr/15/bank-of-england-owned-599-slaves-in-1770s-new-exhibition-reveals

Jordan, C. A. (2007). Rhizomorphics of race and space: Ghana's slave castles and the roots of african diaspora identity. *Journal of Architectural Education* , 60(4), 48–59. JSTOR. https://www.jstor.org/stable/40480850

Karenga, M. (2002). *Introduction to Black studies*. University Of Sankore Press.

Keith, L. (2008, February 22). *The Colfax Massacre*. https://www.c-span.org/program/book-tv/the-colfax-massacre/183520

Keith, L. (2011, March 15). *Colfax Massacre*. 64 Parishes. https://64parishes.org/entry/colfax-massacre

Kellerman, C. J. (2023, February 15). *Slavery and the Catholic Church: It's time to correct the historical record*. America Magazine. https://www.americamagazine.org/faith/2023/02/15/catholic-church-slavery-244703

Kimberley, M. (2020). Prejudential : black America and the presidents. Steerforth Press.

King, J. (2024, May 29). *Research Guides: Emory University and Slavery: Institutional Records*. Guides.libraries.emory.edu; Emory University. https://guides.libraries.emory.edu/c.php?g=1364162&p=10076965

Klan-in-Gainesville. (2007). [Online image]. In *Wikimedia Commons*. https://commons.wikimedia.org/wiki/File:Klan-in-gainesville.jpg

Klein, C. (2016, May 24). *10 Things You May Not Know About Nat Turner's Rebellion*. HISTORY. https://www.history.com/news/10-things-you-may-not-know-about-nat-turners-rebellion

Klein, J. (2010). D.W. Griffith's star on the Hollywood Walk of Fame [Online Image]. In *Wikimedia Commons*. https://commons.wikimedia.org/wiki/File:DW_Griffith_star_HWF.JPG

Koger, L. (1985). Black slaveowners : free Black slave masters in South Carolina, 1790-1860. Mcfarland.

Larson, K. C. (2019). *Harriet Tubman Myths and Facts*. Harriettubmanbiography.com. http://www.harriettubmanbiography.com/harriet-tubman-myths-and-facts.html

Law Insider. (2024, June 5). *Perishable commodities Definition*. Law Insider. https://www.lawinsider.com/dictionary/perishable-commodities#:~:text=Perishable%20commodities%20means%20products%20of

Lawless, J. (2023, January 31). *Church of England sheds light on "shameful" slave trade ties*. AP News. https://apnews.com/article/anglicanism-religion-dd656463d44d6348750d57cc6c91c0c7#

Lee Hayes May. (2018). *The Three P's: Papyrus, Parchment and Paper | Rare Books & Manuscripts*. Www.adelaide.edu.au. https://www.adelaide.edu.au/library/special/exhibitions/cover-to-cover/papyrus/#:~:text=Although%20not%20paper%20in%20the

Leffler, W. K. (1967). Boarded up and damaged buildings on a street after riots in Newark, New Jersey. In *Library of Congress*. https://www.loc.gov/item/2024640675/

Levisay, M. (2014). CSX 2513 (15774966962) [Online image]. In *Wikimedia Commons*. https://commons.wikimedia.org/wiki/File:CSX_2513_(15774966962).jpg

Levs, J. (2020, June 5). They're dragging out the "absent black fathers" myth again. Can we give it a rest? | Opinion. Newsweek. https://www.newsweek.com/absent-black-fathers-myth-racism-1509085

Lewis, J. F. (2011). Arabslavers [Online image]. In *Wikimedia Commons*. https://commons.wikimedia.org/wiki/File:Arabslavers.jpg

Liberato, R. (2007). All Giza pyramids in one shot [Online Image]. In *Wikimedia Commons*. https://commons.wikimedia.org/wiki/File:All_Gizah_Pyramids.jpg

Library Company of Philadelphia. (1836). Middle Passage: Instruments of restraint and torture [Online Image]. In *The Library Company of Philadelphia*. https://digital.librarycompany.org/islandora/object/Islandora%3A2746. (cropped).

Library of Congress. (2014). Letter to the Warring Tribes [Online image]. In *Library of Congress*. https://www.loc.gov/item/2021667540

Library of Congress. (2024). Black sharecropper picking cotton, Chatham County, North Carolina, 8a40861 [Online image]. In *Wikimedia Commons*. https://commons.wikimedia.org/wiki/File:Black_sharecropper_picking_cotton,_Chatham_County,_North_Carolina,_8a40861.tif

Little, B. (2017, August 16). *How the Nazis Were Inspired by Jim Crow | HISTORY*. HISTORY. https://www.history.com/articles/how-the-nazis-were-inspired-by-jim-crow

Litwack, L. F. (1979). Been in the storm so long : the aftermath of slavery. Knopf.

Litwack, L. F. (1998). Trouble in mind : Black southerners in the age of Jim Crow. Vintage Books.

Lloyd's of London. (2015). Lloyd's insurance exterior at night [Online image]. In *Wikimedia Commons*. https://commons.wikimedia.org/wiki/File:Lloyd%27s_insurance_exterior_at_night.jpg

Lockhart, P. R. (2019, August 16). *How slavery became the building block of the American economy*. Vox; Vox. https://www.vox.com/identities/2019/8/16/20806069/slavery-economy-capitalism-violence-cotton-edward-baptist

Logan, R. (1969). The betrayal of the Negro, from Rutherford B. Hayes to Woodrow Wilson, by Rayford W. Logan. Collier Books.

Lomotey, K. (2010). National association of teachers in colored schools. In K. Lomotey (Ed.), *Encyclopedia of African American Education* (pp. 477–478). SAGE Publications, Inc.,; Sage. https://sk.sagepub.com/ency/edvol/africanamericaneducation/chpt/national-association-teachers-colored-schools

Macabasco, L. W. (2022, March 8). Lynching Postcards: a harrowing documentary about confronting history. *The Guardian.* https://www.theguardian.com/film/2022/mar/08/lynching-postcards-a-harrowing-documentary-about-confronting-history

Manning Marable. (1983). How capitalism underdeveloped Black America. South End Pr.

Manning, P. (2007). *The Atlantic slave trade : Effects on economies, societies, and peoples in Africa, the Americas, and Europe* (S. L. Engerman & J. E. Joseph E, Eds.; pp. 117–144). Duke Univ. Press. https://www.google.com/books/edition/The_Atlantic_Slave_Trade/abvkqNGSTZ0C?hl=en&gbpv=1

Maryland Center for History and Culture. (2020, December 7). A Stain on an All-American Brand: How Brooks Brothers Once Clothed Slaves. YouTube. https://www.youtube.com/watch?v=Xr7sCHMeJYM

Massachusetts Office of Travel and Tourism. (2024, December 11). *A Cornerstone of Black History: African Lodge No. 459's 250th Anniversary - MA250.* MA250. https://massachusetts250.org/a-cornerstone-of-black-history-african-lodge-no-459s-250th-anniversary/

Matthews, S., & Florida State College at Jacksonville. (2021). Life as a Slave in the Cotton Kingdom. *Fscj.pressbooks.pub.* https://fscj.pressbooks.pub/africanamericanhistory/chapter/life-as-a-slave-in-the-cotton-kingdom/

McGuire, D. (2024). *Black Women, Civil Rights and the Struggle for Bodily Integrity.* Www.civilrightsmuseum.org. https://www.civilrightsmuseum.org/50-voices-for-50-years/posts/black-women-civil-rights-and-the-struggle-for-bodily-integrity

McGuire, D. L. (2011). At the Dark End of the Street : Black Women, Rape, and Resistance- a New History of the Civil Rights Movement from Rosa Parks to the Rise of Black Power. Vintage Books.

McInnis, M., Batson, B., Crawford, G., & Kimball, G. (2014). *The Auction · To Be Sold: Virginia and the American Slave Trade · Online Exhibitions.* Www.virginiamemory.com. https://www.virginiamemory.com/online-exhibitions/exhibits/show/to-be-sold/eyre-crowe/the-auction

McIntyre, J. B. H. (2023, June 16). *How a Grad Student Uncovered the Largest Known Slave Auction in the U.S.* ProPublica. https://www.propublica.org/article/how-grad-student-discovered-largest-us-slave-auction

Mcpherson, J. M. (1988). Battle cry of freedom : the civil war era. Oxford University Press.

McRae, E. G. (2018a). Mothers of Massive Resistance (Kirtsten Potter, Narrator) (Audiobook). Oxford University Press.

McRae, E. G. (2018b, February 17). *When White Segregationist Women Hated on Eleanor Roosevelt*. The Daily Beast. https://www.thedailybeast.com/when-white-segregationist-women-hated-on-eleanor-roosevelt

Metropolitan Museum of Art. (2023). *Heilbrunn Timeline of Art History*. Metmuseum.org; The Metropolitan Museum of Art. https://www.metmuseum.org/toah/ht/02/afe.html

Miao, N. (2021, March 18). *Building names on campus reflect Vanderbilt's history with slavery, segregation and civil rights - The Vanderbilt Hustler*. The Vanderbilt Hustler. https://vanderbilthustler.com/2021/03/18/building-names-on-campus-reflect-vanderbilts-history-with-slavery-segregation-and-civil-rights/

Michael, J. (2021, October 11). *A Stain on an All-American Brand | Vestoj*. Vestoj.com. https://vestoj.com/how-brooks-brothers-once-clothed-slaves/

Mintz, S. (2019). *Historical Context: Facts about the Slave Trade and Slavery*. The Gilder Lehrman Institute of American History. https://www.gilderlehrman.org/history-resources/teacher-resources/historical-context-facts-about-slave-trade-and-slavery

Mireille Harper. (2021). The Black History Book: Big Ideas Simply Explained. Dk Publishing (Dorling Kindersley).

Mitchell, E. A. (2023, September 4). *How Far Back Were Africans Inoculating Against Smallpox? Really Far Back*. Slate. https://slate.com/news-and-politics/2023/09/smallpox-inoculation-history-onesimus-mather.html

Montero, D. (2024, February 9). *How Wall Street Funded Slavery*. TIME. https://time.com/6692434/wall-street-slavery-essay/

Montgomery Improvement Association. (1956). Flyer posted by the Montgomery Improvement Association of Montgomery, Alabama, regarding desegregated seating in buses. [Online image]. In *Wikimedia Commons*. https://commons.wikimedia.org/wiki/File:Montgomery_Improvement_Association,_flyer_on_bus_desegregation,_c._1956_(NYPL).jpg

Mor, E., Shachnow, L., & Tannenbaum, S. (2023, July 19). *The oldest public school in the US had enslaved people on its campus*. GBH. https://www.wgbh.org/news/local/2023-07-19/the-oldest-public-school-in-the-us-had-enslaved-people-on-its-campus

Morain, D. (2002, May 2). *Slave Owners and Their Insurers Are Named*. Los Angeles Times. https://www.latimes.com/archives/la-xpm-2002-may-02-me-slavery2-story.html

Morgan, E. S. (1975). American Slavery, American Freedom. W. W. Norton & Company.

Mount Vernon Ladies' Association. (2024). *Slave Labor*. George Washington's Mount Vernon. https://www.mountvernon.org/library/digitalhistory/digital-encyclopedia/article/slave-labor/

Movement for Black Lives. (2025). *About us – M4BL*. M4BL. https://m4bl.org/about-us/

Muhammad, K. G. (2019, August 14). The Barbaric History of Sugar in America. *The New York Times*. https://www.nytimes.com/interactive/2019/08/14/magazine/sugar-slave-trade-slavery.html

Muhammad, T. (1996, March 26). *Brief History on Origin of the Nation of Islam*. NOI.org Official Website. https://noi.org/noi-history/

Mulroy, C. (2022, November 4). *The richest person who ever lived had unimaginable wealth. Inside the world's wealthiest*. USA TODAY. https://www.usatoday.com/story/money/2022/11/04/richest-person-ever/10391344002/

Mustakeem, S. M. (2016). Slavery at Sea: Terror, Sex, and Sickness in the Middle Passage. University Of Illinois Press.

NAACP. (2025). *Our history*. Naacp.org; NAACP. https://naacp.org/about/our-history

NASA, ESA and G. Bacon (STScI). (2005). Sirius A and B artwork [Online image]. In *Wikimedia Commons*. https://commons.wikimedia.org/wiki/File:Sirius_A_and_B_artwork.jpg

National Archives. (2019). *Eyewitness*. Archives.gov. https://www.archives.gov/exhibits/eyewitness/html.php?section=2

National Archives. (2021, June 28). *The Great Migration (1910-1970)*. National Archives; The U.S. National Archives and Records Administration. https://www.archives.gov/research/african-americans/migrations/great-migration

National Domestic Workers Alliance. (2021, August 24). *Demanding justice: A history of domestic workers*. Vimeo. https://vimeo.com/591844100

National Geographic. (2016). The First Monotheistic Pharaoh | The Story of God. In *YouTube*. https://www.youtube.com/watch?v=BgFqKXgmv6U

National Park Service. (2005). English flintlock blunderbuss [Online image]. In *Wikimedia Commons*. https://commons.wikimedia.org/wiki/File:English_flintlock_blunderbuss.jpeg

National Park Service. (2022, November 8). *African Americans and the Railroad - Great Smoky Mountains National Park (U.S. National Park Service)*. Www.nps.gov. https://www.nps.gov/grsm/learn/historyculture/african-americans-and-the-railroad.htm#:~:text=Due%20to%20the%20railroad

National Park Service. (2023, August 13). African American railroad workers - Golden Spike National Historical Park (U.S. National Park Service). Www.nps.gov. https://www.nps.gov/gosp/learn/historyculture/african-american-railroad-workers.htm

National Urban League. (2020). *Mission and History*. Nul.org. https://nul.org/mission-and-history

NBC News. (2017). Black rights fugitive JoAnne Chesimard in Cuba - part 2 | NBC News [TV Broadcast]. In *YouTube*. Black Rights Fugitive JoAnne Chesimard In Cuba - Part 2 | NBC News

Northup, S. (2009). *12 Years a Slave*. Digireads.com . (Original work published 1853)

Not Even Past. (2011, November 14). *Daina Ramey Berry on Slave Plantation Life*. YouTube; University of Texas at Austin. https://www.youtube.com/watch?v=_sQQLSUJFR4&t=685s

NPR. (2008, April 29). *America's First Slaves: Whites*. NPR; NPR. https://www.npr.org/transcripts/90034279

NPR. (2018, April 11). Housing Segregation and Redlining in America: A Short History | Code Switch | NPR. YouTube. https://youtu.be/O5FBJyqfoLM?si=8IP97PlMgf9qV1Xq

NPR. (2021, June 2). Historian uncovers the racist roots of the 2nd amendment. NPR. https://www.npr.org/transcripts/1002107670

Nunn, N. (2017, February 27). *Understanding the long-run effects of Africa's slave trades*. CEPR. https://cepr.org/voxeu/columns/understanding-long-run-effects-africas-slave-trades

O'Hagan, S. (2022, September 4). Sisters of the revolution: the women of the Black Panther Party. *The Guardian*. https://www.theguardian.com/artanddesign/2022/sep/04/sisters-revolution-women-of-black-panther-party

Oberlin College. (2021). *Niagaramain*. Oberlin.edu. https://www2.oberlin.edu/external/EOG/Niagara%20Movement/niagaramain.htm

Olaudah Equiano. (2014). Interesting Narrative of The Life Of Olaudah Equiano Or Gustavus Vassa, Th. Harper Collins.

Orfield, G., & Pfleger, R. (2024). *The Unfinished Battle for Integration in a Multiracial America -from Brown to Now*. The Civil Rights Project/Proyecto Derechos Civiles, UCLA. https://www.civilrightsproject.ucla.edu/research/k-12-education/integration-and-diversity/the-unfinished-battle-for-integration-in-a-multiracial-america-2013-from-brown-to-now/National-Segregation-041624-CORRECTED-for.pdf

Packard, J. M. (2002). American nightmare : the history of Jim Crow. St. Martin's Griffin.

Parks, G. (1942). A. Philip Randolph, portrait, November 1942 [Online image]. In *Wikimedia Commons*. https://commons.wikimedia.org/wiki/File:A._Phillip_Randolph_(November_1942).jpg. Gordon Parks for Office of War Information.

PBS. (2017). *Sharecropping | slavery by another name*. Sharecropping | Slavery by Another Name Bento | PBS; PBS. https://www.pbs.org/tpt/slavery-by-another-name/themes/sharecropping/

PBS. (2019a). Africans in America | Part 1 | Narrative | Europeans Come to Western Africa. Pbs.org. https://www.pbs.org/wgbh/aia/part1/1narr1.html

PBS. (2019b). Africans in America | Part 1 | Narrative | The African Slave Trade and the Middle Passage. Pbs.org. https://www.pbs.org/wgbh/aia/part1/1narr4.html

Pearson, S. (2018, September 11). Perspective | Birth certificates have always been a weapon for white supremacists. *Washington Post.* https://www.washingtonpost.com/outlook/2018/09/11/birth-certificates-have-always-been-weapon-white-supremacists/

Phillip, A. (2015, April 15). A permanent reminder of Wall Street's hidden slave-trading past is coming soon. *Washington Post.* https://www.washingtonpost.com/news/morning-mix/wp/2015/04/15/a-permanent-reminder-of-wall-streets-hidden-slave-trading-past-is-coming-soon/

Phillips, J. (1789). Description of a slave ship, 1789 [Online image]. In *Wikimedia Commons.* https://commons.wikimedia.org/wiki/File:Description_of_a_Slave_Ship,_1789.jpg

Plummer, J. (2017). Cape Coast Castle Ghana [Online image]. In *SmugMug.com.* https://plummerphotos.smugmug.com/Travel/GHANA-2017/Ghana-Trip-Day-4-8312017/i-zp7hjmg/A

Plummer, J. (2020). *Sumo Wrestlers & Supermodels.* Plummer Media & Entertainment.

Pollard, S. (Director). (2012). *Slavery by another name* (J. L. Pollard, Ed.). Twin Cities Public Television, Inc.

Price, L. (2024, February 21). *University of Maryland publishes report on school's connections to slavery.* Baltimore Sun. https://www.baltimoresun.com/2024/02/21/university-of-maryland-slavery-report/

Princeton University. (2024). *Racialized Frontiers: Slaves and Settlers in Modernizing Brazil | Brazil LAB.* Brazillab.princeton.edu. https://brazillab.princeton.edu/research/racialized_frontiers#:~:text=Brazil%20was%20built%20on%20the

Raines, H. (1977). My soul is rested movement days in the deep South remembered. Penguin Books.

Ransby, B. (2010, May 3). *Henry Louis Gates' Dangerously Wrong Slave History - Colorlines.* Colorlines. https://colorlines.com/article/henry-louis-gates-dangerously-wrong-slave-history/

Rediker, M. (2007). The Slave Ship: a Human History. Penguin.

Reid, T. (2024). *The Slave Trade Economy & Yale | The Yale & Slavery Research Project.* Ysrp.yale.edu; Yale University. https://ysrp.yale.edu/slave-trade-economy-yale

Rice University. (2010, August 17). "Mitochondrial Eve": Mother of all humans lived 200,000 years ago. ScienceDaily. https://www.sciencedaily.com/releases/2010/08/100817122405.htm

Riddle, L. (2015, March 29). *Clemson's past hides in plain sight*. The Greenville News. https://www.greenvilleonline.com/story/news/local/2015/03/29/clemsons-past-hides-plain-sight/70549126/

Robinson, M. (2023, January 23). *Lone survivor of Birmingham church bombing shares her story at Auburn's annual Dr. Martin Luther King Jr. Scholarship Breakfast*. Office of Communications and Marketing. https://ocm.auburn.edu/newsroom/news_articles/2023/01/231327-mlk-week-scholarship-breakfast.php

Rodney, W. (1981). How Europe Underdeveloped Africa. Howard University Press.

Rosenau, W. (2013). "Our Backs Are Against the Wall": The Black Liberation Army and Domestic Terrorism in 1970s America. *Studies in Conflict & Terrorism, 36*(2), 176–192. Taylor & Francis. https://www-tandfonline-com.proxy.libraries.rutgers.edu/doi/full/10.1080/1057610X.2013.747074

Rotimi, C. N., Tekola-Ayele, F., Baker, J. L., & Shriner, D. (2016). The African Diaspora: History, Adaptation and Health. *Current Opinion in Genetics & Development, 41*, 77–84. https://doi.org/10.1016/j.gde.2016.08.005

Rugendas, J. M. (2020). Johann Moritz Rugendas in Brazil 2 [Online image]. In *Wikimedia Commons*. https://commons.wikimedia.org/wiki/File:Johann_Moritz_Rugendas_in_Brazil_2.jpg

Sales, W. W. (1994). From civil rights to black liberation : Malcolm X and the organization of Afro-American unity. South End Press, Cop.

Sandweiss, M. A., & Hollander, C. (2024). *Princeton and Slavery: Holding the Center*. Slavery.princeton.edu. https://slavery.princeton.edu/stories/princeton-and-slavery-holding-the-center

Saraiva, C. (2021, March 18). Four Numbers That Show the Cost of Slavery on Black Wealth Today. *Bloomberg.com*. https://www.bloomberg.com/news/articles/2021-03-18/pay-check-podcast-episode-2-how-much-did-slavery-in-u-s-cost-black-wealth

Saunders, Z. (2023, October 18). *The LAPD vs. Black Panther Party shootout of Dec. 8, 1969*. San Francisco Bay View. https://sfbayview.com/2023/10/the-lapd-vs-black-panther-party-shootout-of-dec-8-1969/?utm_source=chatgpt.com

Scarlet and Black Research Center. (2024). *Scarlet and Black Research Center, Rutgers University» Slavery Timeline*. Scarlet and Black Research Center, Rutgers University; Rutgers University. https://scarletandblack.rutgers.edu/slavery-timeline/

Schomberg Centre for Research in Black Culture. (2011). Booker T Washington portrait [Online image]. In *Wikimedia Commons*. https://commons.wikimedia.org/wiki/File:Booker_T_Washington_portrait.jpg

Schomburg Center for Research in Black Culture. (1967). A button supporting the campaign to release Huey P. Newton, founder of the Black Panther Party. [Online image]. In *Wikimedia Commons*. https://commons.wikimedia.org/wiki/File:%22Free_Huey,_Seize_the_Time%22_political_button.jpg

Schomburg Center for Research in Black Culture, Manuscripts, Archives and Rare Books Division, The New York Public Library. (1839). A woman with iron horns and bells on, to keep her from running away [Online image]. In *The New York Public Library Digital Collections Digital Collections*. https://digitalcollections.nypl.org/items/510d47da-749c-a3d9-e040-e00a18064a99

School of Pan African Thought. (2016, August 3). Lessons from the Songhai Empire - Everyday Life in an Early African Empire. YouTube. https://youtu.be/LvLWcTJqJXM?si=l92lE3VdlOBCKxcg

Schuessler, J. (2020, December 9). Johns Hopkins Reveals That Its Founder Owned Slaves. *The New York Times*. https://www.nytimes.com/2020/12/09/arts/johns-hopkins-slavery-abolitionist.html

SCLC. (2024, September 18). *SCLC Timeline | National SCLC*. National SCLC. https://nationalsclc.org/sclc-timeline/

Sebastian, L. (2012). Malaita, Solomon Island [Online image]. In *Wikimedia Commons*. https://commons.wikimedia.org/wiki/File:Malaita,_Solomon_Island_(23275239206).jpg

Sheppard, W. L. (2017). William L. ShepparFirst use of the Cotton Gin, Harper's weekly, 18 Dec. 1869, p. 813 [Online image]. In *Wikimedia Commons*. https://commons.wikimedia.org/wiki/File:William_L._Sheppard_-_First_use_of_the_Cotton_Gin,_Harper%27s_weekly,_18_Dec._1869,_p._813.png

Sieff, K. (2018, January 29). An African Country Reckons with its History of Selling Slaves. *The Washington Post*. https://www.washingtonpost.com/world/africa/an-african-country-reckons-with-its-history-of-selling-slaves/2018/01/29/5234f5aa-ff9a-11e7-86b9-8908743c79dd_story.html

Sisters, G. (2020). Ota Benga at 1904 World's Fair [Online image]. In *Wikimedia Commons*. https://commons.wikimedia.org/wiki/File:Ota_Benga_at_1904_World%27s_Fair.jpg

Slave Voyages Consortium. (2021). *Slave voyages*. Slavevoyages.org. https://www.slavevoyages.org

Smallwood, S. E. (2022). Saltwater Slavery : A Middle Passage from Africa to American Diaspora. Harvard University Press.

Smith, S. (2015, February 10). *Black Confederates: Truth and Legend.* American Battlefield Trust. https://www.battlefields.org/learn/articles/black-confederates-truth-and-legend

Smithsonian National Museum of African American History and Culture. (2021). Freedmen's School, James Plantation, North Carolina [Online image]. In *Wikimedia Commons.* https://commons.wikimedia.org/wiki/File:Freedmen%27s_School,_James_Plantation,_North_Carolina.png

Stack, L. (2017, March 17). Debunking a Myth: The Irish Were Not Slaves, Too. *The New York Times.* https://www.nytimes.com/2017/03/17/us/irish-slaves-myth.html

Stampp, K. (1956). The peculiar institution : slavery in the ante-bellum South. Vintage Books.

Stannard, D. E. (1992). American holocaust : the conquest of the New World. Oxford University Press.

Stearns, J. B. (2019). Junius Brutus Stearns - George Washington as Farmer at Mount Vernon [Online image]. In *Wikimedia Commons.* https://commons.wikimedia.org/wiki/File:Junius_Brutus_Stearns_-_George_Washington_as_Farmer_at_Mount_Vernon.jpg

Stewart, J. C. (1996). 1001 things everyone should know about African American history. Gramercy Books.

Stoper, E. (1977). The Student Nonviolent Coordinating Committee. *Journal of Black Studies, 8*(1), 13–34. https://doi.org/10.1177/002193477700800102

Supreme Understanding. (2013). When the World Was Black Part One. Supreme Design Publishing.

Swarns, R. (2016, April 16). 272 Slaves Were Sold to Save Georgetown. What Does It Owe Their Descendants? *The New York Times.* https://www.nytimes.com/2016/04/17/us/georgetown-university-search-for-slave-descendants.html

Swedish Army Museum. (2012). M1 carbine, USA. caliber .30 carbine [Online image]. In *Wikimedia Commons.* https://commons.wikimedia.org/wiki/File:M1_Carbine_Mk_I_USA_Arm%C3%A9museum_noBG_new.png

Tensley, B. (2021). *Black voting rights and voter suppression: A timeline.* Www.cnn.com. https://www.cnn.com/interactive/2021/05/politics/black-voting-rights-suppression-timeline/

Terrell, E. (2023, June 27). *Research Guides: This Month in Business History: Brotherhood of Sleeping Car Porters Union Formed.* Guides.loc.gov. https://guides.loc.gov/this-month-in-business-history/august/brotherhood-of-sleeping-car-porters

Thomas, Z. (2019, August 29). The hidden links between slavery and Wall Street. *BBC News.* https://www.bbc.com/news/business-49476247

Trichon, A. (1883). Révolte sur un navire négrier [Online image]. In *Wikimedia Commons*. https://commons.wikimedia.org/wiki/File:R%C3%A9volte_sur_un_navire_n%C3%A9grier.jpg

Turnbull, H. (2020). *Women in resistance*. Miami.edu. https://scholar.library.miami.edu/slaves/womens_resistance/individual_essays/harmony.html

Turner, C. (Director). (2021, November 22). *Lynching Postcards: Token of a Great Day*. MTV Documentary Films.

United States Library of Congress. (1863). African American soldier in Union uniform with wife and two daughters (cropped) [Online image]. In *Wikimedia Commons*. African American soldier in Union uniform with wife and two daughters (cropped)

United States National Advisory Commission on Civil Disorders. (1968). *Report of the National Advisory Commission on Civil Disorders*. U.S. Department of Housing and Urban Development (HUD). https://www.hud.gov/sites/dfiles/FHEO/documents/kerner_commission_full_report.pdf

University of Mississippi Graduate School. (2020). *Uncovering the Stories of Enslaved Persons at the University of Mississippi*. Graduate School. https://gradschool.olemiss.edu/newsletter-fall-winter-2020/uncovering-the-stories-of-enslaved-persons-at-the-university-of-mississippi/

University of Virginia Library. (2016, March 18). *Universities Studying Slavery*. President's Commission on Slavery and the University. https://slavery.virginia.edu/universities-studying-slavery/

Until Freedom. (2025). *About | Until Freedom*. About Us. https://untilfreedom.com/about/

Vachon, J. (1941). Negro carrying sign in front of milk company. Chicago, Illinois [Online image]. In *Library of Congress*. https://www.loc.gov/resource/fsa.8c19566/

Virginia Archives. (2015). VA health bulletin [Online image]. In *Wikimedia Commons*. https://commons.wikimedia.org/wiki/File:Va_health_bulletin.jpg

Wake Forest University Slavery, Race and Memory Project. (2024). *The Slavery, Race and Memory Project*. Slavery, Race and Memory Project; Wake Forest University. https://srmp.wfu.edu

Walker, C. E. (1992). "When I Can Read My Title Clear": Literacy, Slavery, and Religion in the Antebellum South. *The Journal of American History, 79*, 262–264.

Walker, R. (2013). Blacks and science. Volume 3, African American contributions to science and technology. Createspace.

Walker, R. (2015). If You Want to Learn Early African History Start Here. CreateSpace.

Washington, H. A. (2006). Medical Apartheid: The Dark History of Medical Experimentation on Black Americans from Colonial Times to the Present. Paw Prints.

WashU & Slavery Project. (2024). *The WashU & slavery project*. The WashU & Slavery Project. https://slavery.wustl.edu

Weidman, B. (2016, August 15). *Black Soldiers in the U.S. Military During the Civil War*. National Archives. https://www.archives.gov/education/lessons/blacks-civil-war#:~:text=By%20the%20end%20of%20the

Wellcome Images. (2014). L0057128 Cat-o-nine tails, United Kingdom, 1700-1850 [Online image]. In *Wikimedia Commons*. https://commons.wikimedia.org/wiki/File:Cat-o-nine_tails,_United_Kingdom,_1700-1850_Wellcome_L0057128.jpg

Wells-Barnett, I. B. (2020). Crusade for justice : the autobiography of Ida B. Wells (A. Duster, Ed.). The University of Chicago Press.

White House Historical Association. (2024). *Slavery in the President's neighborhood FAQ*. WHHA (En-US). https://www.whitehousehistory.org/slavery-in-the-presidents-neighborhood-faq

White, B. (2016, October 21). *Honoring The Women Of The Black Panther Party*. Essence. https://www.essence.com/holidays/black-history-month/women-black-panther-party/#77169

White, D. G. (1999). Ar'n't I a woman? : female slaves in the plantation South. Peter Smith.

Wilder, C. S. (2014). Ebony and ivy : race, slavery, and the troubled history of America's universities. Bloomsbury Press.

Wilder, C. S., Alapati, V., Beauchemin, L., Diaz, M., Fisher, Z., Heins, O., Kortman, L., Meles, A., Nadeem, M., Pakuwal, I., Wong, M., Beiruti, S., Eduzor, C., Geathers, D., George, M., George, M., Alexander, A., Elango, M., & Murphy, N. (2020). *Slavery and the founding of MIT*. MIT & Slavery; MIT Libraries. https://digital-exhibits.libraries.mit.edu/s/mit-and-slavery/page/slavery-and-the-founding-of-mit

Wilkerson, I. (2016, September). *The Long-Lasting Legacy of the Great Migration*. Smithsonian; Smithsonian.com. https://www.smithsonianmag.com/history/long-lasting-legacy-great-migration-180960118/

William & Mary. (2024). *The Lemon Project*. William & Mary. https://www.wm.edu/sites/lemonproject/

Williams, N. L. (2025). *NJ Department of State - Historical Commission - Juneteenth 2021*. Nj.gov. https://nj.gov/state/historical/his-2021-juneteenth.shtml

Williams, R. (1979). Eyes on the Prize: America's Civil Rights Years (1954-1965) (Blackside, Inc, Interviewer) [Interview]. In *Washington University Libraries, Film and Media Archive, Henry Hampton Collection*. https://www.crmvet.org/nars/williamr.htm#citation

Williamson, J. (1986). *A Rage for Order*. Oxford University Press.

Wolcott, M. P. (1940). Negro worker who does housework when not picking cotton. [Online image]. In *Library of Congress*. https://www.loc.gov/resource/fsa.8c30715/. Near Natchitoches, Louisiana.

Wolfson, S. (1964). Elijah Muhammad addresses followers including Muhammad Ali / World Telegram & Sun photo by Stanley Wolfson [Online image]. In *Wikimedia Commons*. https://commons.wikimedia.org/wiki/File:Elijah_Muhammad_and_Cassius_Clay_NYWTS.jpg

World Bank Group. (2023, May 23). *Afro-descendants in Latin America:* World Bank. https://www.worldbank.org/en/region/lac/publication/afrodescendants-in-LAC

Yale University. (2020, November 19). Centering the Transatlantic Slave Trade in the Critique of Capital. YouTube. https://youtu.be/o79zdE5JxVo?si=zsES_4sjHsDMfiap

Yanker Poster Collection. (1965). Political prisoners of USA fascism Bobby, Huey. [Online Image]. In *Library of Congress*. https://www.loc.gov/resource/cph.3g06286/

Zapata, C. (2010, March 4). *Great Migration: Definition, Causes & Impact | HISTORY*. HISTORY. https://www.history.com/topics/black-history/great-migration?utm_source=chatgpt.com#impact-of-the-great-migration

Zelasko, K. (2012). This is a redlining map of Chicago, as created by the home owners' loan corporation [Online image]. In *Wikimedia Commons*. https://commons.wikimedia.org/wiki/File:Holc-chicago.jpg

Zinn Education Project. (2016, June 12). *Black Abolitionists - Zinn Education Project*. Zinn Education Project. https://www.zinnedproject.org/materials/black-abolitionists/

Zirkel, K. C. (2018). Flags of the Ivy League fly at Columbia's Wien Stadium [Online image]. In *Wikimedia Commons*. https://commons.wikimedia.org/wiki/File:Flags_of_the_Ivy_League.jpg

Chapter Introduction Photographs

Chapter 1

Corbalan, J. (n.d.). Montessori map of Africa made of wood with countries separated by colors. [Online Image]. In Envato Elements. Retrieved June 2, 2025, from https://elements.envato.com/montessori-map-of-africa-made-of-wood-with-countri-DJHXKKU

Chapter 2

Rawpixel. (n.d.). Woman hands tied up with a rope [Online Image]. In Envato Elements. Retrieved June 2, 2025, from https://elements.envato.com/woman-hands-tied-up-with-a-rope-AWE7H3S

Chapter 3

svetlaya_83. (n.d.). Male hand clenched into a fist. The black life of matter. [Online Image]. In Envato Elements. Retrieved June 2, 2025, from https://elements.envato.com/male-hand-clenched-into-a-fist-the-black-life-of-m-49WZWUQ

Chapter 4

Siegel , A. S. (1942). Detroit, Michigan, 1942: Sign "We want white tenants in our white community," [Online Image]. In Wikimedia Commons. https://commons.wikimedia.org/wiki/File:We_want_white_tenants.jpg

Chapter 5

Plummer, J. I. (2020). My skin is not a crime [Online Image]. In Smugmug. https://www.smugmug.com/%20https://photos.smugmug.com/Protests/6132020-Plainfield-Black-Lives-Matter-Youth-Rally/i-bChV7c8/0/NWvWg4b3QqSB84tBFMxtRfgG5t5smZgGz9XxnX7RJ/D/A9_01799-D.jpg

ABOUT THE AUTHOR

Joel I. Plummer earned a B.A. in African and African American Studies, an M.A. in history, and was inducted into Phi Beta Kappa at Rutgers University-Newark. He earned a Certificate of Supervision of Instruction through the Rutgers University Graduate School of Education. He has taught African American and U.S. history for more than two decades at the secondary level and in the Africana Studies department at Rutgers University in New Brunswick, New Jersey.

In addition to teaching, Joel I. Plummer has been a professional photographer and photojournalist for over a decade. His work has been published by the Los Angeles Times, The Wall Street Journal, The Daily Beast, Newsweek, NBC, CBS, Sports Illustrated, ESPN, and numerous international media outlets. He is a product of the Plainfield Public School District in New Jersey, a member of Iota Phi Theta Fraternity, Inc., and still lives in Plainfield with his wife, Danielle, and their children, Alexis, Morgan, and Mason.

www.ingramcontent.com/pod-product-compliance
Lightning Source LLC
Chambersburg PA
CBHW080342170426
43194CB00014B/2652